QUICK & EASY

DIABETIC MENUS

Betty Wedman, M.S., R.D.

CB

CONTEMPORARY BOOKS

Library of Congress Cataloging-in-Publication Data

Wedman, Betty.
    Quick & easy diabetic menus : more than 150 delicious recipes for
breakfast, lunch, dinner, and snacks / Betty Wedman.
       p.   cm.
    Includes index.
    ISBN 0-8092-3853-5
    1. Diabetes—Diet therapy—Recipes.   I. Title.   II. Title: Quick
and easy diabetic menus.
    RC662.W365   1993
    641.5'6314—dc20   93-13237
                                                CIP

Cover design by Georgene Sainati
Cover photograph by C. C. Cain Photography

Published by Contemporary Books
A division of NTC/Contemporary Publishing Group, Inc.
4255 West Touhy Avenue, Lincolnwood (Chicago), Illinois 60712-1975 U.S.A.
Printed in the United States of America
International Standard Book Number: 0-8092-3853-5
00 01 02 03 04 05 QM 28 27 26 25 24 23 22 21 20 19 18 17 16 15 14 13 12

To my father, Joseph St Louis, who has always been
the most important person in my life

CONTENTS

PREFACE

Welcome to a new look at healthy meals and recipes. This book is designed to provide you with complete menus for the day or a special-occasion meal.

The part of meal planning people dislike the most—aside from washing dishes—is putting the "pieces" of a meal together. Deciding what vegetable and starch to serve with lamb chops or broiled snapper can be frustrating and thankless. When you also have to figure out how many exchanges to include in a meal, menu planning can be a daunting task.

Quick & Easy Diabetic Menus makes both tasks simpler by providing 30 days of delicious menus along with more than 150 recipes. And most of the recipes are simple and easy to fix, though a few more elaborate ones are included for when you want to show off your culinary skills.

In short, here is an effortless way to plan and prepare meals. The hallmark of a nutrition educator is being able to combine nutrition theory and food appeal. Planning meals and combining foods to meet the American Diabetes Association (ADA) recommendations for people with diabetes makes that task an even greater challenge. I hope I have met that challenge in creating these 30 days of meals.

Now is the time to take control of meal planning and stop feeling deprived. Bon appétit.

ACKNOWLEDGMENTS

Many thanks to all the dedicated food and nutrition professionals who have influenced my nutrition career. They instilled in me the desire to search for goals beyond recipe development.

Special thanks to Contemporary Books for believing in the concept of a diabetes cookbook like this and giving me the opportunity to produce it.

INTRODUCTION

American Diabetes Association Nutritional Recommendations

Following appropriate nutritional guidelines is very important for people with diabetes. Therefore, this chapter begins with a summary of the ADA's current recommendations. Also crucial to good health is exercise; its incorporation into a healthy eating plan is reviewed briefly here, too.

Planning what to eat and when and then preparing it quickly and easily are the keys to sound diabetic nutrition. And because it all starts with a well-stocked pantry, this chapter also provides helpful tips on buying food, as well as handling and storing it safely. Finally, you'll find some ideas for brown-bagging, for advance preparation and freezing of recipes, and other hints that can make meal planning and preparation for those with busy lives an easier and more pleasant job.

The ADA identifies the nutritional goals for diabetes management as

- maintaining blood glucose (sugar) as close to normal (80–120 mg/dl) as possible
- taking in adequate nutrients (calories, protein, vitamins, and minerals) for growth and repair of body tissues

1

- timing meals and snacks consistently to prevent blood glucose (sugar) swings from high to low
- managing weight

Meal plans featured in *Quick & Easy Diabetic Menus* adhere to the ADA principles of good nutrition in diabetes:

- Using high-fiber foods as a primary source of carbohydrates—whole grains, fruits, and vegetables
- Stressing low-fat ingredients, particularly avoiding saturated fat, to reduce risks of hyperlipidemia since a higher rate of coronary heat disease has been identified in those with diabetes
- Keeping sodium levels moderate
- Using sugar (sucrose) minimally in recipes—amounts do not exceed the ADA 1 teaspoon per serving. Recipes you may have that contain more than 1 teaspoon but less than 1 tablespoon of sugar per serving are considered for "occasional use"—no more than one a day. Recipes using more than 1 tablespoon of sugar per serving are generally not recommended. Sucrose, as opposed to other sweeteners, is used in recipes because of its high acceptability and low cost.

The recipes and menus in *Quick & Easy Diabetic Menus* offer a wide variety of foods that are high in fiber, low in fat, low in sodium, and low in sugar.

Alternative sweeteners such as aspartame and saccharin can be used in beverages. The use of caloric sweeteners—fructose and sorbitol—is not recommended *unless* the calories are counted into the meal plan.

Alcohol may be consumed based on advice from the physician and/or diabetes educator but should be used in moderation. One ounce of alcohol is the amount in a 1½-ounce shot of distilled liquor, a 4-ounce glass of wine, or a 12-ounce can or bottle of beer. Light beer and dry wine are usually identified as better choices because they have less carbohydrate content than regular beer and sweet wine.

Alcoholic beverages are best consumed *with* meals or snacks. Do not omit foods from the meal plan to make up the caloric difference with an alcoholic beverage. This practice could lead to hypoglycemia.

Exercise: Part of the Nutritional Plan

Research has shown that exercise improves digestion, nutrient utilization, bowel function, and physical stamina. In diabetes management, in fact, exercise is just as important as meal planning. Muscle tone, a sense of well-being, and controlled body weight are all reasons to keep an active exercise regimen in your daily life.

Those with diabetes need to plan exercise into their daily regimens just as they do meals.

Exercise one to two hours after a meal for the best control of blood glucose. If you want to exercise before breakfast, you'll need to eat one starch/bread food (12–15 grams of carbohydrate) before exercising.

Testing blood glucose levels before and after exercise can provide a good guide to how much food you need to compensate for calories burned during exercise. Activities lasting over an hour or vigorous exercise like swimming, soccer, basketball, and cycling usually create a need for extra food. Activities like snow skiing, scuba diving, marathons, and swim meets will require you to consume more calories than are in the usual meal plan.

Here is a rule of thumb to use in planning extra caloric consumption:

> Less than one hour of exercise—
> Add one starch/bread (15
> grams of carbohydrate).

> One hour of exercise—Add one
> starch/bread and one protein.
> More than one hour of exercise—
> Add one starch/bread, one
> protein, and one fruit.

High-intensity exercise like ice skating, hockey, racquetball, and shoveling heavy snow may require you to consume two starch/bread, two protein, and one milk before starting.

Hypoglycemia or insulin reaction/low blood sugar may occur in people with diabetes who are on insulin or taking oral hypoglycemic agents. In that case the 15/15 rule is recommended for treatment: Consume 15 grams of carbohydrate—1 tablespoon honey or ½ cup fruit juice or ½ cup regular soft drink—which can raise the blood glucose 50–100 mg/dl. Fifteen minutes later, do a blood glucose monitoring test. If the blood glucose is under 80 mg/dl, consume another 15 grams of carbohydrate.

Adequate hydration or fluids during exercise is also important. Water is the best fluid to consume for the first hour of any exercise. Water regulates body temperature and moves nutrients to cells throughout the body to be burned for energy. Sweating during exercise results in even greater losses of fluid from the body.

Thirst may not be an indicator of fluid needs on a hot, humid day or during heavy exercise. Drink water regularly during these times to reduce fatigue and prevent heat stress.

Consume 1 cup of water for every hour of exercise to ensure adequate hydration. The most accurate way to determine *your* hydration needs is to weigh yourself before and after exercise. Drink 2 cups of water for every pound of body weight lost.

"Sports drinks" with added sugar (glucose, fructose, and/or sucrose) may be considered for activities lasting longer than 1 hour. Many of these products have electrolytes—potassium, sodium, and chloride—in a sugar solution. Avoid drinks that contain more than 10 percent sugar. They may cause cramping, nausea, and bloating unless diluted with water. Regular soft drinks are 12 percent sugar and create gastric problems for many athletes.

Because exercise improves the body's use of insulin and thereby lowers blood glucose (sugar) levels, more calories may need to be added to the meal plan.

Tips for Quick and Easy Meal Preparation

Preparing delicious, healthful meals can be simple as long as you do some planning. An important element is keeping the pantry well stocked with nutritious foods—buying what you'll need ahead of time and then keeping it fresh. A well-stocked pantry helps you reduce waste and avoid numerous last-minute shopping trips. Planning ahead can also lead to more imaginative brown-bag choices.

Stocking a Healthful Pantry

The ADA recommends that complex carbohydrates constitute over 50 percent of your daily food intake. A minimum of refined or "simple" carbohydrates (sugar) is advised. That means whole grains, beans, legumes, and starchy vegetables need to be the major foods in your meal plan.

Fiber, found in beans, legumes, whole grains, fruits, and vegetables, is a necessary part of the daily diet. To get the recommended 25 to 40 grams of fiber per day, most of your daily calories need to come from starches and grains. Foods like grains, dried beans, and winter squash will stay fresh for months, so it's easy to keep a supply available.

The balance of the calories in your daily diet come from proteins and fats. About 1 gram of protein per kilogram (2.2 pounds) of body weight is needed per day to maintain body growth and repair. Choose low-fat protein sources to keep total calories under control. Fish and skinless poultry are good choices. Ground turkey is a low-fat staple used in many recipes in this book, and using frozen makes it easy to keep on hand.

Keep fat calories under 30 percent of your total caloric intake, and one way to achieve that goal is to buy nonfat or low-fat milk, cottage cheese, and yogurt.

Using vegetable oils rather than butter or other saturated fats in baking and cooking reduces the saturated fat content in your diet. Many of the recipes in this book use oil when butter might be used in a similar recipe. When the recipes do call for margarine or butter, choose a brand that is low in saturated fat.*

How Much Is Enough?

Deciding how much food to buy can be a headache: The chart on the following page offers some basic guidelines to follow in keeping a well-stocked pantry. They can help determine if enough food is available for a family picnic, weekend party, or vacation camping trip.

Food Storage

Who wants to go to the grocery store every day? When most of us have a large refrigerator-freezer at home, those time-consuming errands just aren't necessary. Keeping food fresh is important not only to your health but also to your budget. To make sure your meal preparation is truly quick and easy, learn how to keep food fresh once you purchase it. Here are some tips for keeping your pantry full and minimizing waste.

*References: "Nutritional recommendations and principles for individuals with diabetes mellitus." American Diabetes Association Position Statement. Diabetes Care, vol. 13, supp. 1, 1990. "Effect of isocaloric substitution of chocolate cake for potato in type 1 diabetes patients." A. L. Peters, M. B. Davidson, and K. Eisenbury. Diabetes Care, vol. 13, 1990. "Clinical aspects of sucrose and fructose metabolism." J. P. Bantle. Diabetes Care, vol. 12, 1989.

Foods	To Serve				
	1–2	4–6	10–12	18–20	25+
Lettuce	.5 lb.	2 lb.	4 lb.	6 lb.	8 lb.
Tomatoes	1	2	4	6	8
Onions	1	2	4	6	8
Potatoes	1 lb.	2 lb.	4 lb.	6 lb.	8 lb.
Mustard	2 oz.	6 oz.	12 oz.	18 oz.	24 oz.
Mayonnaise	2 oz.	6 oz.	12 oz.	18 oz.	24 oz.
Catsup	2 oz.	6 oz.	12 oz.	18 oz.	24 oz.
Bread	1 loaf	2 loaves	4 loaves	6 loaves	8 loaves
Chicken (3–3.5 lb.)	1	2	4	6	8
Ground Beef (hamburger)	.5 lb.	1.5 lb.	3 lb.	5 lb.	8 lb.

- Dairy and eggs: Eggs always need to be refrigerated. They keep best in their original cartons instead of a refrigerator egg tray if not used within a week. Egg whites can be frozen for up to a year in small containers for future use in baked goods. Milk needs to be continuously refrigerated. Make the dairy and frozen foods sections your last stop before the checkout, to ensure fresh dairy products. Cheese can be kept in a warmer part of the refrigerator—like a drawer—and is best served at room temperature. Use airtight containers for aromatic cheeses. All cheeses will develop mold if they are stored long enough. If you can't bear to throw the cheese away, freeze it for use in a baked product, cheese soufflé or a baked macaroni and cheese casserole, for example. Do *not* cut off mold that develops on them and use the rest of the cheese. Mold strains go deep into the cheese and can be toxic to the gastrointestinal system. Margarine and butter can be frozen for up to a year, provided heavy plastic paper or freezer bags are used to preserve flavor.

• Meats, poultry, and fish: Fish requires the most careful handling of all the animal protein foods. Fresh fish needs to be cleaned as soon as a selection is made and kept cold constantly to ensure quality and freshness. Buy and use fish and shellfish the same day unless you're going to freeze it. To freeze fish, use a glaze of water to keep it from drying out, submerging fillets in "almost" frozen water. Let stand for 2 minutes, then remove each fish fillet from the water and wrap it in plastic wrap or freezer paper. Place in a heavy-duty freezer bag labeled with the date and type of fish. Use within three months. Shellfish—shrimp, scallops, crab—can be frozen the same as fish. They need to be used within three months to ensure good quality. Fresh meat and poultry should be used within three days or frozen for up to a year. Ground meats should be used within 24 hours or frozen. Keep meat in the coldest part of the refrigerator to minimize bacterial growth. Cured meats, like bacon and ham, can be kept for a week or frozen for a month. To freeze, wrap meats in freezer paper or use a plastic bag. Spread them out on the shelf until frozen solid for fast freezing. Defrost meat and poultry 24 hours ahead of time *in the refrigerator. Never* let meat or poultry thaw at room temperature— all the juices will run out, and bacteria growth can be a problem.

• Fruits and vegetables: Apples, bananas, pears, peaches, and plums, once ripened at room temperature, should be refrigerated in a drawer or plastic container to retain moisture. Even ripe bananas can be stored in the refrigerator. (Banana peel turns dark, but the fruit stays tasty and delicious.) Citrus fruits last two to four weeks in the refrigerator, depending on freshness when purchased. Sprinkle washed carrots and celery with water and place in a loosely wrapped container to allow them to breathe. Lettuce is best used within two days, rinsed under cold running water and spun dry. Store potatoes in a cool, dry, dark place—not in the refrigerator or freezer. Onions can be kept for six to nine months in a cool, dry, dark storage area or refrigerated in a dry spot.

• Other foods: Baked products can be kept in the refrigerator for longer storage. Loosely cover cakes and pastry with foil or plastic wrap. Inverting a bowl over a cake or pastry is another convenient method of storage. Unfrosted baked cakes, muffins, and cookies can be frozen for up to a year. Unbaked cookie batter and piecrusts keep for up to three months in the freezer. Coffee, from whole beans to instant, keeps best in the refrigerator or freezer.

Food Safety

• Cook beef and lamb to medium
• Cook chicken, pork, and fish to well done
• Avoid all raw or undercooked meats
• Throw out eggs with cracked shells
• Boil eggs for at least 7 minutes
• Fry eggs for at least 3 minutes on each side
• Scramble eggs to a dry, not runny, consistency
• Avoid foods with raw eggs
• Use pasteurized milk products
• Use pasteurized cheeses
• Throw moldy cheese away
• Wash all fruits and vegetables well
• Avoid moldy fruits and vegetables

- Use rotating turntable in microwave or turn foods by hand frequently
- Avoid wooden cutting boards
- Clean up knives and cutting boards after preparing raw eggs and meat
- Use dishcloths and towels once before laundering

Meals and Snacks to Take Along

Everyone brown-bags it at some time or another. Having interesting ideas to fit into the meal plan can make these meal-packing chores less bothersome.

- Pack frozen shrimp cocktail (frozen shrimp and cocktail sauce—no lettuce). Within three to four hours it will be defrosted and ready to eat with crackers and fruit dessert.
- Stir wheat germ and fresh fruit into yogurt for lunch. Instant coffee can also be added as flavoring.
- Stuff a tomato with tuna or chicken salad.
- Turn plain low-fat cottage cheese into a garden salad by stirring chopped cucumbers, radishes, and celery into it.
- Make a yogurt cheese sandwich spread (see Index) for use on bread or crackers.
- Keep a supply of crackers, melba toast, raisins, sunflower seeds, dried fruit, and wheat germ in a desk drawer. Make interesting new food combinations by using these with other packable foods.

MENUS

Food Groups for Easy Menu Planning

Different groups of foods provide different nutrients. Menu planning is easier when you know which foods fit into each group.

- *Fruits*: provide vitamin C, folic acid, potassium, and sometimes vitamin A.
- *Vegetables*: provide Vitamin A, folic acid, potassium, and some Vitamin C and iron.
- *Starches and Grains (bread)*: provide thiamine, niacin, pyroxidine, iron, selenium, and some protein, magnesium, and manganese.
- *Dairy Products*: provide calcium, riboflavin, phosphorus, and protein.
- *Meat, Poultry, and Seafoods*: provide protein, zinc, iron, and selenium.
- *Fats*: provide fat-soluble vitamins A and E.

The American Diabetes Association divides foods into six food groups, based on *carbohydrate* content. Some foods like cheese are included not in the milk group but in the protein group (except cream cheese, which is considered a fat).

Each serving—also known as an *exchange* or *choice*—
of a food in the following groups contains the amount of
carbohydrate listed.

• Starch/Bread: 15 g
• Fruit: 10 g
• Vegetable: 5 g
• Milk (*not* cheese): 12 g
• Protein: 0
• Fat: 0

Basic   Menu   Guide

The menus were planned using six food groups that repre-
sent foods with similar carbohydrate content and nutrient
values. Each breakfast, lunch, and dinner has similar calorie
and carbohydrate content.

Breakfast
Menus contain about 350–400 calories and feature this meal
pattern:

    2 starch/bread servings
    1–2 fruit servings
    1 low-fat protein *or* milk serving
    1–2 fat servings

Lunch
Menus contain about 450–500 calories and feature this meal
pattern:

    2 starch/bread servings
    1 fruit serving
    1 vegetable serving
    2–3 protein servings *or* 2 protein
        + 1 milk serving
    1–2 fat servings

Dinner

Menus contain about 550–600 calories and feature this meal pattern:

2 starch/bread servings*
1 fruit serving
1-2 vegetable servings
3-4 protein servings
1-2 fat servings

Because interesting food combinations and menus do not fit perfectly into the six food groups, there will be some "substitutions" made in the Breakfast, Lunch, and Dinner menus. These are some of the substitutions found when totalling up the food exchanges in the menus that follow.

1 fruit may be substituted for 1
    starch/bread
1 starch/bread may be substituted
    for 1 milk
1 starch/bread may be substituted
    for 1 fruit
1 milk may be substituted for 1
    protein
1 protein may be substituted for 1
    milk (especially for those
    people with lactose
    intolerance)

These substitutions keep the calories and carbohydrate content about the same so should have minimum effect on blood sugar (blood glucose) management.

Some menus include a food group—like fat or a starch/bread—that has been "borrowed" from the next meal or previous meal. Food exchanges and menu guides are only a helpful way to put foods together to make an interesting,

*May vary from 1-3 servings based on other foods served at meal.

tasty, and nutritious meal. Casseroles, stews, and desserts don't always come out to the *exact* food exchanges planned for a breakfast, lunch, or dinner. So "borrowing" between meals allows for an increased use of many recipes.

Snacks

Snacks have 100–125 calories per serving and usually feature a carbohydrate and protein or fat combination:

    1 starch/bread serving
    1 fat serving
    or
    1 fruit serving
    1 protein or milk serving

Each recipe in *Quick & Easy Diabetic Menus* provides, per serving, the nutritional analysis, as well as the number of exchanges from each food group. For example: 1 Crunchy Oat Bran Muffin = 1 starch/bread + 1 fat.

The menus in this chapter conform to the ADA patterns for each meal. Should you wish to substitute another recipe for one listed, simply choose one with the same exchanges to stay within the guidelines for that meal.

Basic Menu Serving Sizes

The menus in this book include some items that have no corresponding recipe. For those items, each portion should equal the basic serving size as stated in the ADA's *Exchange Lists for Meal Planning*, reprinted on the following pages.

Starch/Bread List

CEREALS/GRAINS/PASTA

Bran cereals, concentrated . . . . ⅓ cup
Bran cereals, flakes (such as
    Bran Buds, All-Bran) . . . . ½ cup

Bulgur (cooked) .... ½ cup
Cooked cereals .... ½ cup
Cornmeal (dry) .... 2½ tablespoons
Grape-Nuts .... 3 tablespoons
Grits (cooked) .... ½ cup
Other ready-to-eat unsweetened cereals . ¾ cup
Pasta (cooked) .... ½ cup
Puffed cereal .... 1½ cups
Rice, white or brown (cooked) .... ⅓ cup
Shredded wheat .... ½ cup
Wheat germ .... 3 tablespoons

DRIED BEANS/PEAS/LENTILS

Beans and peas such as kidney, white,
    split, black-eyed (cooked) .... ½ cup
Lentils (cooked) .... ⅓ cup
Baked beans .... ¼ cup

STARCHY VEGETABLES

Corn .... ½ cup
Corn on cob, 6 inches long 1
Lima beans .... ½ cup
Peas, green .... ½ cup
Plantain .... ½ cup
Potato, baked .... 1 small (3 ounces)
Potato, mashed .... ½ cup
Squash, winter (acorn, butternut) ..... ¾ cup
Yam, sweet potato, plain .... ⅓ cup

BREAD

Bagel .... ½ (1 ounce)
Breadsticks, crisp, 4 inches long by ½
    inch .... 2 (⅔ ounce)
Croutons, low-fat .... 1 cup
English muffin .... ½
Frankfurter or hamburger bun .... ½ (1 ounce)
Pita, 6 inches across .... ½

Plain roll, small......................1 (1 ounce)
Raisin, unfrosted.....................1 slice (1 ounce)
Rye, pumpernickel ....1 slice (1 ounce)
Tortilla, 6 inches across..............1
White (including fresh, Italian) ....1 slice (1 ounce)
Whole-wheat ....1 slice (1 ounce)

CRACKERS/SNACKS

Animal crackers 8
Graham crackers, 2½-inch square 3
Matzo ....¾ ounce
Melba toast ....5 slices
Oyster crackers 24
Popcorn (popped, no fat added) ....3 cups
Pretzels...........................¾ ounce
Ry-Krisp, 2 inches by 3½ inches 4
Saltine-type crackers 6
Whole-wheat crackers, no fat added
    (crisp breads, such as Finn Crisp,
    Kavli, Wasa) ....¾ ounce

STARCH FOODS PREPARED WITH FAT
(Count as 1 starch/bread serving plus 1 fat serving.)

Biscuit, 2½ inches across 1
Chow mein noodles ....½ cup
Corn bread, 2-inch cube ....1 (2 ounces)
Cracker, round butter type 6
French fried potatoes, 2 inches to 3½
    inches long ....10 (1½ ounces)
Muffin, plain, small 1
Pancake, 4 inches across..............2
Stuffing, bread (prepared)............¼ cup

Protein List

One, two, or three servings of meat or other protein may be eaten depending on whether at breakfast, lunch, or dinner. This list divides meats and other protein foods by fat content. The weight listed is the cooked or ready-to-eat size.

LOW-FAT PROTEIN

Beef: USDA good or choice grades
of lean beef, such as round, sirloin,
and flank steak; tenderloin; and
chipped beef ....1 ounce
Pork: Lean pork, such as fresh ham;
canned, cured, or boiled ham;
Canadian bacon; tenderloin ....1 ounce
Veal: All cuts are lean except for veal
cutlets (ground or cubed).
Examples of lean veal are chops
and roasts.......................1 ounce
Poultry: Chicken, turkey, Cornish hen
(without skin) ....1 ounce
Fish: All fresh and frozen fish ....1 ounce
Crab, lobster, scallops, shrimp, clams,
(fresh or canned in water) ....2 ounces
Oysters ....6 medium
Tuna (canned in water)...............¼ cup
Herring (uncreamed or smoked) ....1 ounce
Sardines (canned) ....2 medium
Wild Game: Venison, rabbit, squirrel ...1 ounce
Pheasant, duck, goose (without skin) ...1 ounce
Cheese: Any cottage cheese ....¼ cup
Grated Parmesan ....2 tablespoons

Diet cheeses (with fewer than 55
        calories per ounce)...............1 ounce
Other: 95% fat-free luncheon meat .....1 ounce
Egg whites 3
Egg substitutes with less than 55
        calories per ¼ cup ....¼ cup

MEDIUM-FAT PROTEIN

Beef: Most beef products fall into this
        category. Examples are all ground
        beef, roast (rib, chuck, rump), steak
        (cubed, porterhouse, T-bone), and
        meat loaf.......................1 ounce
Pork: Most pork products fall into this
        category. Examples are chops, loin
        roast, Boston butt, cutlets. ....1 ounce
Lamb: Most lamb products fall into this
        category. Examples are chops, leg,
        and roast......................1 ounce
Veal: Cutlet (ground or cubed,
        unbreaded) ....1 ounce
Poultry: Chicken (with skin), domestic
        duck or goose (well drained of fat),
        ground turkey ....1 ounce
Fish: Tuna (canned in oil and drained) .¼ cup
Salmon (canned) ....¼ cup
Cheese: Skim or part-skim milk cheeses,
        such as:
Ricotta ....¼ cup
Mozzarella ....1 ounce
Diet cheeses (with 56–80 calories per
        ounce) ....1 ounce
Other: 86% fat-free luncheon meat .....1 ounce
Egg (high in cholesterol, limit to 3 per
        week) ....1 ounce

Egg substitutes with 56–80 calories per
   ¼ cup ....¼ cup
Tofu (2½ inches by 2¾ inches by 1
   inch) ....4 ounces
Liver, heart, kidney, sweetbreads
   (high in cholesterol)..............1 ounce

HIGH-FAT PROTEIN

Remember, these items are high in saturated fat, cholesterol, and calories and should be used only 3 times per week.

Beef: Most USDA prime cuts of beef,
   such as ribs, corned beef ....1 ounce
Pork: Spareribs, ground pork, pork
   sausage (patty or link)............1 ounce
Lamb: Patties (ground lamb) ....1 ounce
Fish: Any fried fish product............1 ounce
Cheese: All regular cheeses, such as
   American, blue, cheddar, Monterey
   Jack, Swiss ....1 ounce
Other: Luncheon meat, such as
   bologna, salami, pimiento loaf .....1 ounce
Sausage, such as Polish, Italian ....1 ounce
Knockwurst, smoked ....1 ounce
Bratwurst ....1 ounce
Frankfurter (turkey or chicken) ....1 frank
                     (10 per pound)

Peanut butter
   (contains unsaturated fat).........1 tablespoon

Count as 1 high-fat meat plus 1 fat exchange:
   Frankfurter (beef, pork, or
   combination)....................1 frank
                     (10 per pound)

Vegetable List

The serving size for vegetables is:
½ cup cooked vegetables or vegetable juice
1 cup raw vegetables

Artichoke (½ medium)   Mushrooms
Asparagus   Okra
Beans (green, wax, Italian)   Onions
Bean sprouts   Pea pods
Beets   Peppers (green)
Broccoli   Rutabaga
Brussels sprouts   Sauerkraut
Cabbage   Spinach
Carrots   Summer squash (crookneck)
Cauliflower   Tomato (1 large)
Eggplant   Tomato/vegetable juice
Greens (collard, mustard,   Turnips
    turnip)   Water chestnuts
Kohlrabi   Zucchini
Leeks

Starchy vegetables such as corn, peas, and potatoes are
found on the Starch/Bread List.

FRUIT LIST

The serving size for fruit is usually:
½ cup fresh fruit
½ cup fruit juice
¼ cup dried fruit

Fruits vary in carbohydrate and calorie count, so here is
a detailed listing of the most commonly eaten ones and the
amount for 1 serving.

FRESH, FROZEN, AND UNSWEETENED CANNED FRUIT

Apple (raw, 2 inches across)...........1
Applesauce (unsweetened) ....½ cup

Apricots (medium, raw) 4
Apricots (canned) ....½ cup or 4 halves
Banana (9 inches long) ....½
Blackberries (raw) ....¾ cup
Blueberries (raw) ....¾ cup
Cantaloupe (5 inches across) ....⅓ melon or
           1 cup cubes
Cherries (large, raw) 12
Cherries (canned) ....½ cup
Figs (raw, 2 inches across) ....2 figs
Fruit cocktail (canned) ....½ cup
Grapefruit (medium) ....½
Grapefruit (segments) ....¾ cup
Grapes (small) 15
Honeydew melon (medium) ....⅛ melon or
           1 cup cubes
Kiwifruit (large)....................1
Mandarin oranges ....¾ cup
Mango (small)......................½
Nectarine (1½ inches across)..........1
Orange (2½ inches across)............1
Papaya ....1 cup
Peach (2¾ inches across) 1
Peaches (canned) ....½ cup or 2 halves
Pear...............................½ large or 1 small
Pears (canned) ....½ cup or 2 halves
Persimmon (medium, native) 2
Pineapple (raw)....................¾ cup
Pineapple (canned) ....⅓ cup
Plum (raw, 2 inches across) 2
Pomegranate ....½
Raspberries (raw) ....1 cup
Strawberries (raw, whole) ....1¼ cups
Tangerine (2½ inches across) 2
Watermelon (cubes) ....1¼ cups

DRIED FRUIT

Apples............................4 rings
Apricots ....7 halves
Dates............................2½ medium
Figs 1½
Prunes ....3 medium
Raisins ....2 tablespoons

FRUIT JUICE

Apple juice/cider ....½ cup
Cranberry juice cocktail ....⅓ cup
Grapefruit juice......................½ cup
Grape juice ....⅓ cup
Orange juice ....½ cup
Pineapple juice ....½ cup
Prune juice ....⅓ cup

Milk List

Milk and milk products are divided into three parts based on the amount of fat and calories in them.

SKIM AND VERY LOW-FAT MILK

Skim milk ....1 cup
½% milk...........................1 cup
1% milk ....1 cup
Low-fat buttermilk ....1 cup
Evaporated skim milk ....½ cup
Dry nonfat milk ....⅓ cup
Plain nonfat yogurt.................8 ounces

LOW-FAT MILK

2% milk ....1 cup
Plain low-fat yogurt (with added nonfat
    milk solids) ....8 ounces

WHOLE MILK

Whole Milk ....1 cup
Evaporated whole milk...............½ cup
Plain whole yogurt ....8 ounces

Fat List

The foods listed vary in serving sizes.

UNSATURATED FATS

Avocado ....⅛ medium
Margarine ....1 teaspoon
Margarine, diet ....1 tablespoon
Mayonnaise ....1 teaspoon
Mayonnaise, reduced-calorie...........1 tablespoon
Nuts and Seeds:
Almonds, dry-roasted................6 whole
Cashews, dry-roasted ....1 tablespoon
Peanuts............................20 small or
                                   10 large
Pecans ....2 whole
Walnuts............................2 whole
Other nuts ....1 tablespoon
Pine nuts ....1 tablespoon
Sunflower seeds (without shells).......1 tablespoon
Pumpkin seeds ....2 teaspoons
Oil (corn, cottonseed, safflower,
     soybean, sunflower, olive, peanut)..1 teaspoon
Olives ....10 small or
                                   5 large
Salad dressing, mayonnaise-type ....2 teaspoons
Salad dressing, mayonnaise-type,
reduced calorie ....1 tablespoon
Salad dressing (all varieties)...........1 tablespoon
Salad dressing, reduced-calorie ....2 tablespoons
(Two tablespoons of fat free salad dressing is a free food.)

SATURATED FATS

Butter ....1 teaspoon
Bacon ....1 slice
Chitterlings ....½ ounce
Coconut, shredded ....2 tablespoons
Coffee whitener, liquid ....2 tablespoons
Coffee whitener, powder ....4 teaspoons
Cream (light, coffee, table)...........2 tablespoons
Cream, sour.......................2 tablespoons
Cream (heavy, whipping) ....1 tablespoon
Cream cheese ....1 tablespoon
Salt pork..........................¼ ounce

The following 30-day menu plans will give you a wide variety
of suggested dishes for breakfast, lunch, dinners and snacks.
After selecting your choice of menu for the day, you can find
the accompanying recipes by refering to the index. Following these are a selection of special menues featuring vegetarian, Jewish and holiday fare.

M e n u 1

Breakfast	Crunchy Oat Bran Muffin*
	Bran cereal
	Low-fat milk
	Banana slices
Lunch	Turkey Waldorf Salad*
	Ry-Krisp
	Sliced tomatoes
Dinner	Mexican Flank Steak*
	Pineapple Cheddar Rice*
	Green beans
	Dinner roll
	Peach Melba*
Snack	Zucchini Carrot Bar*

*See Index for recipe.

Menu 2

Breakfast   Banana French Toast*
                             Reduced-calorie syrup
                             Low-fat milk

Lunch   Taco Pie*
                             Tossed salad
                             Almost Zero Salad
                                  Dressing*
                             Orange slices

Dinner   Cranberry Cooler*
                             Creole Flounder*
                             Noodles
                             Peas and carrots
                             Oriental Cabbage Salad*

Snack   Popcorn

*See Index for recipe.

M e n u   3

Breakfast
                               Pecan Waffle*
Reduced-calorie syrup
Canadian bacon
Orange juice

Lunch
                               Broccoli Cheese Soup*
Bran Muffin*
Cottage cheese and apple
    slices on lettuce

Dinner
                               Ham Steak with Mustard
    Pineapple Sauce*
Baked sweet potato
Sautéed zucchini
Mandarin Orange Spinach
    Salad*
Tapioca Pudding*

Snack
                               Chocolate Chip Snack
    Cake*

*See Index for recipe.

Menu 4

Breakfast	Bran Muffin*
	Fruit-flavored low-fat yogurt
Lunch	Tuna Rice Casserole*
	Tossed salad
	Low-fat salad dressing
	Baked Apple*
Dinner	Baked Chicken Parmesan*
	Baked sweet potato
	Steamed cabbage
	Tomato and cucumber salad
	Blueberry Crumble*
Snack	Banana Nut Bread*

*See Index for recipe.

Menu 5

Breakfast   Corn Muffin*
                         Bran cereal
                         Low-fat milk
                         Sliced strawberries

Lunch   Vegetable soup
                         Hot German Chicken Salad*
                         Greek Potato Salad*
                         Fresh fruit garnish

Dinner   Lobster Newburg*
                         Noodles
                         Zucchini Medley*
                         Grapefruit Delight*

Snack   Crunchy Cereal Bar*

*See Index for recipe.

M e n u 6

Breakfast   Date Nut Roll*
                   Low-fat milk

Lunch   Taco Salad*
                   Fruit Compote*
                       with Strawberry
                       Topping*

Dinner   Seafood Scampi*
                   Rice
                   Frosted Cauliflower*
                   Strawberry Salad*
                   Frozen yogurt

Snack   Guiltless Brownies*

*See Index for recipe.

M e n u   7

Breakfast	Bran cereal
	Low-fat milk
	Peach slices
	Raisin toast
	Margarine or butter
Lunch	Hearty Vegetarian Chili*
	Saltines
	Summer Delight Salad*
Dinner	Pork Chops in Orange
	Ginger Sauce*
	Savory Herbed Potatoes*
	Green beans
	Vegetable salad
	Almost Zero Salad
	Dressing*
	Sponge Cake with
	Strawberries*
Snack	Applesauce Brownie*

*See Index for recipe.

Menu 8

Breakfast	Banana French Toast*
	Reduced-calorie syrup
	Low-fat milk
Lunch	Zesty Chef's Salad*
	Melba toast
	Orange juice
Dinner	Florida Herbed Scallops*
	Brown rice
	Steamed asparagus
	Biscuit
	Grated carrot and raisin
	salad
Snack	Hummus*
	Carrot and celery sticks

*See Index for recipe.

M e n u 9

Breakfast	Zucchini Carrot Muffin* Low-fat yogurt
Lunch	Barley Pecan Salad* Low-fat mozzarella cheese sticks Mixed fruit cup
Dinner	Broiled chicken Baked potato Brussels sprouts Mixed vegetable salad Almost Zero Salad Dressing* Vanilla ice milk
Snack	Baked Custard*

*See Index for recipe.

Menu 10

Breakfast   Pecan Waffle*
                         Applesauce
                         Low-fat milk

Lunch   Spinach Rice Casserole*
                         Corn bread square
                         Apricot halves

Dinner   Shrimp Curry*
                         Rice
                         Steamed broccoli
                         Heart of lettuce salad
                         Fat-free salad dressing
                         Melon cubes

Snack   Polish Poppy Seed Bread*
                         Margarine

*See Index for recipe.

M e n u 1 1

Breakfast

Oatmeal
Low-fat milk
Bagel
Margarine
Orange juice

Lunch

Hot Scallops on Romaine
    Salad*
Corn muffin*
Apple wedges

Dinner

Vegetable Spaghetti Sauce*
Noodles
Grated Parmesan cheese
Italian blend vegetables
Hard roll
Grapefruit half

Snack

Strawberry Cantaloupe
    Cooler*
Graham crackers

*See Index for recipe.

Menu 12

Breakfast   Crunchy Oat Bran Muffin*
                          Bran cereal
                          Raisins
                          Low-fat milk

Lunch   Deep-Dish Pizza*
                          Pear

Dinner   Broiled Macadamia Tuna
                              Delight*
                          Boiled potatoes with parsley
                          Sautéed zucchini and
                              onions
                          Mandarin Orange Spinach
                              Salad*

Snack   Rice Pudding*

*See Index for recipe.

Menu 13

Breakfast

Pancakes
Reduced-calorie syrup
Low-fat milk

Lunch

Smoked salmon on bagel
Cream cheese
Gingered Fruit*

Dinner

Chicken Cassoulet*
Coleslaw
Peach Melba*

Snack

Cinnamon Crunch Snack
    Mix*

*See Index for recipe.

Menu 14

Breakfast	Scones* Reduced-calorie fruit spread Low-fat milk
Lunch	Prosciutto Honeydew melon Zucchini Carrot Muffin
Dinner	Minestrone* Dilly Corn Muffin* Cottage cheese and peach slices
Snack	Carrot Bundt Cake*

*See Index for recipe.

Menu 15

Breakfast	Oatmeal
	Low-fat milk
	Banana slices
Lunch	Mulligatawny Soup*
	Hearty Oatmeal Bread*
	Orange slices
Dinner	Vegetarian Lasagna*
	Mixed greens
	Low-Fat Thousand Island
	Dressing*
	Pear slices
Snack	Chocolate Carrot Cake*

*See Index for recipe.

Menu 16

Breakfast   Pancakes
                   Applesauce
                   Low-fat milk

Lunch   Turkey Quiche*
                   Corn muffin*
                   Fresh fruit garnish

Dinner   Grilled lamb chops
                   Brown rice
                   Broccoli spears
                   French Bread Pudding*

Snack   Purple Passion*
                   Graham crackers

*See Index for recipe.

Menu 17

Breakfast   Waffle
                                   Canadian bacon
                                   Strawberry Topping*

Lunch   Frosty Peach Nog*
                                   Sliced turkey sandwich
                                   Pickles and olives

Dinner   New England Halibut Stew*
                                   Mixed vegetable salad
                                   Low-Fat Thousand Island
                                        Dressing*
                                   Spritz Cookie*

Snack   Zesty Corn 'n' Nuts*

*See Index for recipe.

Menu 18

Breakfast   Oatmeal
                           Raisins
                           Low-fat milk
                           English muffin half
                           Margarine or butter

Lunch   Spinach Barley Casserole*
                           Sunflower Loaf*
                           Peach and banana slices

Dinner   Cornish Hen with Apple
                               Stuffing*
                           Peas and carrots
                           Seven-Layer Vegetable
                               Salad*
                           Melon cubes

Snack   Carrot Muffin*

*See Index for recipe.

M e n u   1 9

Breakfast	Banana Chocolate Muffin*
	Low-fat yogurt
Lunch	Cheese Soufflé*
	Polish Poppy Seed Bread*
	Spinach Apple Salad*
Dinner	Cinnamon Apple Pork Tenderloin*
	Scalloped Potatoes*
	Asparagus
	Dinner roll
	Orange slices
Snack	Bran Cereal
	Low-fat milk

*See Index for recipe.

Menu 20

Breakfast	Tofu Peanut Butter–Oatmeal Cookie*
	Low-fat milk
Lunch	Impossible Taco Pie*
	Corn bread square
	Tropical Splash*
Dinner	Greek Meatballs*
	Rice
	Baked acorn squash
	Green beans
	Cream-Filled Strawberries*
Snack	Cinnamon Crunch Snack Mix*

*See Index for recipe.

Menu 21

Breakfast   Abelskiver Pancakes*
Reduced-calorie syrup
Low-fat milk

Lunch   Sliced ham sandwich
Pickles and olives
Pineapple cubes

Dinner   Chicken Legs and Sweet
Potatoes*
Brussels Sprouts with
Almonds*
Cucumber and tomato salad
Frozen yogurt

Snack   Applesauce Brownie*

*See Index for recipe.

Menu 22

Breakfast   Poached egg
                          Whole-wheat toast
                          Margarine
                          Grapefruit juice

Lunch   Gazpacho Cocktail*
                          Tuna salad sandwich
                          Fresh fruit cup

Dinner   Roasted turkey breast
                          Baked Vegetable Medley*
                          Mixed vegetable salad
                          Almost Zero Salad
                                Dressing*
                          Poached Pears with
                                Chocolate Sauce*

Snack   Pumpkin Pudding Cake*

*See Index for recipe.

Menu 23

Breakfast	Grilled ham
	Raisin toast
	Margarine or butter
Lunch	Pizza Salad*
	Carrot Muffin*
	Fresh pear
Dinner	Bankruptcy Stew*
	Spinach Apple Salad*
	Rice Pudding*
Snack	White Chocolate
	Macadamia Cookie*

*See Index for recipe.

Menu 24

Breakfast   Cocoa Muffin*
                       Low-fat milk

Lunch   New England Clam
                           Chowder*
                       French bread
                       Cheese
                       Grapes

Dinner   Cornish Hen with Raspberry
                           Sauce*
                       Lima Beans and Tomatoes*
                       Asparagus spears
                       Dinner roll
                       Fresh fruit cup

Snack   Oatmeal Cookie*

*See Index for recipe.

M e n u 2 5

Breakfast   Oatmeal
                             Sliced banana
                             Low-fat milk
                             Whole-wheat toast

Lunch   Sautéed Salmon Spinach
                                 Salad*
                             Corn muffin*
                             Melon wedges

Dinner   Brunswick Stew*
                             Mixed vegetable salad
                             Low-Fat Thousand Island
                                 Dressing*
                             Swedish Fruit Soup*

Snack   Granola Bar*

*See Index for recipe.

Menu 26

Breakfast   Ricotta cheese
                   Bagel
                   Grapefruit half

Lunch   Baba Ghanouj*
                   Raw vegetables
                   English Pea Salad*
                   Whole-wheat roll
                   Margarine
                   Apricot halves

Dinner   Fish Fillets with Grapefruit*
                   Rice
                   Orange Dill Carrots*
                   Summer Delight Salad*
                   Gingerbread Cookie*

Snack   Sponge Cake with
                        Strawberries*

*See Index for recipe.

M e n u   2 7

Breakfast	Prune Orange Breakfast Roll*
	Low-fat yogurt
Lunch	Red Cabbage and Apple Soup*
	Cold plate (sliced ham and turkey)
	Sweet Potato Salad*
Dinner	Broiled lamb chops
	Baked potato
	Broiled Tomato with Pesto*
	Sliced cucumber
	Gingered Fruit*
Snack	Macadamia Pound Cake*

*See Index for recipe.

Menu 28

Breakfast	Bran cereal
	Low-fat milk
	Sliced strawberries
	Raisin toast
Lunch	Fresh Fruit Gazpacho*
	Cottage cheese
	Hard roll
	Margarine
Dinner	Baked Cornish hen
	Peas and carrots
	Mixed vegetable salad
	Almost Zero Salad
	Dressing*
	Banana Rum Cocktail*
Snack	Zucchini Cupcake*

*See Index for recipe.

Menu 29

Breakfast	Scrambled egg
	Prune Bread*
	Margarine or butter
Lunch	Pasta Vegetable Salad*
	Part-skim mozzarella cheese
	cubes
	Apple slices
Dinner	Baked pork chops
	Red Cabbage with Raisins*
	Peas and onions
	Carrot and celery sticks
	French Bread Pudding*
Snack	Applesauce Brownies*

*See Index for recipe.

Menu 30

Breakfast   Turkey-Sausage Sandwich*
                             Orange juice

Lunch   Vegetable Juice Cocktail*
                             Sliced turkey
                             Roman Sandwich Bread*
                             Grapes

Dinner   Lentil Spaghetti Sauce*
                             Noodles
                             Green beans
                             Baked Bananas in
                                 Strawberry Sauce*

Snack   Peanut Butter Chocolate
                                 Chip Cookies*

*See Index for recipe.

Special Menus

Vegetarian Menus

Vegetarian recipes are found throughout *Quick & Easy Diabetic Menus*. Some are lacto-ovo-vegetarian dishes* like Cheesy Vegetable Loaf, Kidney Bean Cheese Dip, and Cheese Soufflé. Other recipes feature legumes (dried beans) in new ways, like Lentil Spaghetti Sauce, Bean Burgers, Hearty Vegetarian Chili, and Hummus.

Here are some menus for the different types of vegetarian eating styles.

*Lacto-ovo vegetarian includes eggs and dairy products.

Lacto-Ovo-Vegetarian

(Milk and milk products, eggs, whole grains, nuts, and legumes are consumed as protein sources.)

Breakfast	Grapefruit half
	Bulgur cereal
	Low-fat milk
	Whole-grain toast
	Peanut butter
Lunch	Cheesy Vegetable Loaf*
	Bran muffin*
	Sliced tomato
	Fresh fruit
Dinner	Vegetarian Lasagna*
	Green beans
	Whole-grain bread
	Banana half
	Low-fat milk
Snack	Oatmeal Cookie*

*See Index for recipe.

Lacto-Vegetarian

(Dairy products, whole grains, nuts, and legumes are consumed as protein sources, but not eggs.)

Breakfast   Grapefruit half
                             Bulgur cereal
                             Milk
                             Whole-grain toast
                             Peanut butter

Lunch   Cheesy Vegetable Loaf*
                             Whole-grain bread
                             Sliced tomato
                             Fresh fruit

Dinner   Bean Burger*
                             Green beans
                             Banana half

Snack   Granola Bar*

*See Index for recipe.

Vegan

(Whole grains, nuts, and legumes are consumed as protein sources. Soy milk and soy cheese [tofu] are substituted for cow's milk and cheese.)

Breakfast   Grapefruit half
                         Bulgur cereal
                         Soy milk
                         Whole-grain toast
                         Peanut butter

Lunch   Bean Burger*
                         Sliced tomato
                         Fresh fruit

Dinner   Lentil Spaghetti Sauce*
                         Noodles
                         Green beans
                         Whole-grain garlic bread
                         Banana half

Snack   Granola Bar*

*See Index for recipe.

Kosher Meals

Some people of Jewish faith may observe kosher diet principles throughout the year; others may use kosher menus only
during Passover or other special occasions.

Both dairy meals and meat meals can be planned using
Quick & Easy Diabetic Menus. The menus are not kosher
for Passover if flour products are used. Matzo crackers can be
used in the meal instead of leavened quick breads.

Dairy Menus

Vegetarian Lasagna*	Cheese Soufflé*	Ricotta Cassata*
Garlic toast	English Pea Salad*	Green beans
Garden salad	Hearty Oatmeal Bread*	Strawberry Salad*
Fresh fruit cup	Grapefruit half	Peanut Butter Cookie*

Meat Menus

Chicken Legs and Sweet Potatoes*	Mexican Flank Steak*	Cornish Hen with Raspberry Sauce*
Brussels sprouts	Brown Rice	Baked potato
Dinner roll	Spinach	Broccoli Salad with Vinaigrette Dressing*
Orange Ambrosia*	Dinner roll	Whole-grain bread
Granola Bar*	Peach Melba*	Baked Apple*

*See Index for recipe.

Holidays and Celebrations

Holiday meals often turn into an overwhelming display of foods. Concentrate on quality, not quantity, when sampling foods at a holiday celebration.

Plan some exercise among your daily activities to help keep blood glucose under control. Walking in a park or a sports contest in the backyard or basement may encourage group participation.

Mineral water and nonalcoholic wines are festive and can be provided as a substitute for alcoholic beverages.

Recipes in *Quick & Easy Diabetic Menus* can be used to make a healthy holiday meal:

Holiday   Menu

Cranberry Cooler*
Roast turkey
Baked sweet potato
Banana Nut Bread*
Brussels sprouts
Seven-Layer Vegetable
      Salad*
Macadamia Pound Cake*

*See Index for recipe.

M i c r o w a v e   M e n u s

Here are several microwave recipes that have been combined
into meals.

Breakfast	Date Nut Roll*
	Low-fat yogurt
Lunch	Taco Salad*
Dinner	Baked Chicken Parmesan*
	Zucchini Medley*
	Savory Herbed Potatoes*
	Garden salad and dressing
	Blueberry crumble*

or

Dinner	Seafood Scampi*
	Dinner roll
	Frosted Cauliflower*
	Coleslaw
	Grapefruit Delight*
Snack	Crunchy Cereal Bar*
	Sugar-free lemonade

*See Index for recipe.

Sick-Day Menu

No one seems to be able to avoid getting colds, the flu, and viruses. Preparation for these "sick days" starts *before* illness occurs. Have these foods in the pantry for those emergency times:

>Instant cooked cereal
>Ready-to-eat tapioca pudding
>Canned soup
>Canned fruit juices, unsweetened
>Popsicles
>Applesauce, unsweetened

Breakfast	Orange juice
	Cooked cereal
	Low-fat milk
Mid-Morning	½ twin Popsicle
Lunch	Canned soup
	Apple juice or applesauce
	Scrambled egg
Midafternoon	Tapioca pudding
Dinner	Canned soup
	Poached egg on toast
	Orange juice
Bedtime	½ twin Popsicle

Be sure to add 1 cup water or diet soft drink every hour when blood glucose is over 240 mg/dl.

Dental Soft Menu

At some point in life, dental work may require you to eat a "dental soft menu." This menu features foods that do not require chewing before being swallowed.

Recipes are provided for the menu items.

Breakfast   Banana Smoothy*
                             Cooked cereal

Lunch   Chicken noodle soup
                             Cottage cheese
                             Tapioca Pudding*

Dinner   Chicken noodle soup
                             Scrambled egg
                             Strawberry Yogurt Drink*

Snack   Ice milk
                             or
                             Baked Custard*

Be sure to add 1 cup water or diet soft drink every hour when blood glucose is over 240 mg/dl.

*See Index for recipe

APPETIZERS

Cherry Tomatoes with Pesto Filling

24 cherry tomatoes
1 teaspoon dried basil leaves
2 tablespoons pine nuts, toasted
1 small clove garlic, minced
1 ounce Parmesan cheese

Cut the tops off the tomatoes and carefully hollow them out. Place the tomatoes on a baking sheet. Combine the other ingredients in a blender or food processor and blend until the cheese and pine nuts are ground.

Stuff the filling into the tomatoes. Refrigerate.

Serve cold or heat in a preheated 400°F oven for 10 minutes before serving.

Makes 6 servings

One serving of 4 tomatoes = 101 calories
3 g protein
8 g carbohydrate
7 g fat
84 mg sodium

One serving = 1 vegetable + 1 fat

Lima Bean – Filled Potato Snacks

1 cup cooked or drained canned
   lima beans
1 clove garlic, minced
1 tablespoon fresh lemon juice
¼ cup chopped yellow onion
1 tablespoon chopped fresh
   parsley
½ teaspoon dried dill weed
¼ cup plain yogurt
24 new potatoes, cooked

Preheat the oven to 350°F. Combine all the ingredients except the yogurt and new potatoes in a nonstick skillet. Cook over medium heat until the onions are tender, about 5 minutes. Pour into a food processor or blender and add the yogurt. Process until smooth. Cut a thin slice off the bottom of each potato so it will not roll. Scoop out a small amount of potato and fill the cavity with the lima bean mixture. Heat the stuffed potatoes for 10 to 15 minutes before serving.

Makes 6 servings

One serving of 4 potatoes = 187 calories
                          5 g protein
                          32 g carbohydrate
                          2 g fat
                          75 mg sodium

One serving = 2 starch/bread

H u m m u s

1 15-ounce can chick-peas
    (garbanzo beans)
2 tablespoons fresh lemon juice
¼ cup sesame seeds, toasted
¼ cup chopped yellow onion
3 cloves garlic, chopped
2 teaspoons olive oil
2 teaspoons ground cumin
⅛–¼ teaspoon cayenne pepper
½ teaspoon salt (optional)
Chopped fresh parsley for
    garnish

Drain the chick-peas, reserving ¼ to ½ cup of the liquid. Combine all the ingredients except parsley in a blender. Puree until smooth, adding chick-pea liquid if needed to thin the puree. Refrigerate for 3–6 hours before serving to blend the flavors. Garnish with parsley before serving. Serve with vegetables, pita bread, or as sandwich spread.

Makes 1½ cups

One serving of ¼ cup = 111 calories
                 5 g protein
                 8 g carbohydrate
                 6 g fat
                 82 mg sodium

One serving = 1 low-fat protein + 1 fat

B a b a G h a n o u j

1 medium-size eggplant
1 small clove garlic, minced
1 tablespoon tahini (see note)
⅛ teaspoon ground cumin

Preheat the broiler. Slice the eggplant crosswise into ½-inch slices. Place them on a baking sheet and broil 3 inches from the heat until soft and water beads on the surface. Cool and peel the slices, then puree in a blender or food processor along with the rest of the ingredients. Chill and serve with vegetables.

Makes 1 cup

Note: Tahini is sesame paste, made from ground sesame seeds like peanut butter. It's available at health food stores and many supermarkets.
One serving of ⅓ cup = 68 calories
                      3 g protein
                      6 g carbohydrate
                      4 g fat
                      38 mg sodium

One serving = 1 vegetable + 1 fat

Kidney Bean Cheese Dip

1 15- to 17-ounce can red kidney
    beans
2 tablespoons vegetable oil
¼ teaspoon ground cumin
¼ teaspoon garlic powder
2 cups grated cheddar cheese

Drain the beans, reserving the liquid. In a skillet, combine the oil and beans and cook over medium heat, mashing the beans with a wooden spoon or potato masher. After 5 minutes, stir in the cumin and garlic powder. Add the bean liquid and simmer for 10 minutes longer. Remove from the heat and add the cheese. Stir until cheese melts. Serve warm as a dip with fresh vegetables or tortilla chips.

Makes 2 cups

One serving of ½ cup = 319 calories
                    16 g protein
                    32 g carbohydrate
                    13 g fat
                    429 mg sodium

One serving = 1 starch/bread + 2 medium-fat protein + 1 fat

Pimiento Cheese Spread

½ pound cheddar cheese
1 4-ounce jar pimiento pieces
1 cup low-fat cottage cheese
¼ cup mayonnaise

Cut the cheese into strips. Grate in a food processor or blender. Add the rest of the ingredients and process until smooth. Refrigerate until ready to use as a spread on crackers or as stuffing for celery or cherry tomatoes.

Makes 2 cups

One serving of 2 tablespoons = 118 calories
9 g protein
4 g carbohydrate
13 g fat
384 mg sodium

One serving = 1 high-fat protein + 1 fat

T u r k e y   P â t é

1 pound ground turkey
1 small clove garlic, minced
1 small yellow onion, minced
1 teaspoon dried basil leaves
½ teaspoon ground thyme
¼ teaspoon freshly ground white
    pepper
¼ teaspoon salt
1 tablespoon dry sherry or apple
    juice

Sauté the turkey, garlic, onion, basil, and thyme in a non-stick skillet over medium heat until browned. Cool. Spoon the mixture into a food processor or blender. Add the pepper, salt, and sherry and process until the mixture is pureed. Press into a mold or serving bowl. Cover and refrigerate overnight. Serve with crackers or toast points.

Makes 1½ cups

One serving of ¼ cup = 97 calories
                      12 g protein
                      2 g carbohydrate
                      4 g fat
                      294 mg sodium

One serving = 2 low-fat protein

Parmesan Wheat Crackers

1½ cups whole-wheat flour
¼ teaspoon salt
¼ cup cold margarine
2 tablespoons sesame seeds
About ⅓ cup cold water
¼ cup freshly grated Parmesan
    cheese

Preheat the oven to 375°F. Combine the flour and salt in a mixing bowl. Cut in the margarine with a fork or pastry blender until the mixture resembles coarse meal. Sprinkle on the sesame seeds and blend in. Add the water, about 2 tablespoons at a time, until the dough sticks together. Roll out to an ⅛-inch thickness on a floured surface. Sprinkle about one-third of the cheese over half of the dough. Fold the other half of the dough over the cheese; seal the edges of the dough. Roll out again to an ⅛-inch thickness and cut into the desired shapes. Bake on lightly oiled baking sheet for 10–15 minutes. The crackers will be crunchy. If made ahead, keep them in an airtight container or freeze until needed. Recrisp in 350°F oven for 3–5 minutes just before serving.

Makes 18 2-inch crackers

One serving of 3 crackers = 134 calories
                      5 g protein
                      18 g carbohydrate
                      7 g fat
                      269 mg sodium

One serving = 1 starch/bread + 1 fat

SOUPS

New England Clam Chowder

*6 tablespoons margarine or
    butter*
2 cups chopped celery
2 cloves garlic, minced
2 cups chopped yellow onion
¼ cup all-purpose flour
2 cups skim milk
1 cup peeled and diced potatoes
*1 pound fresh or frozen shucked
    clams*
1 tablespoon dried thyme leaves
1 teaspoon salt

Melt 2 tablespoons of the margarine in a skillet. Add the celery, garlic, and onions and sauté over medium heat for 3–5 minutes, until celery is tender. Melt the remaining margarine in large saucepan and stir in the flour. Cook over medium heat for a few minutes, until the mixture starts to brown. Gradually add the skim milk, stirring rapidly to prevent lumps from forming. Add the potatoes and cook for 10 minutes, stirring occasionally. Add the sautéed vegetables, clams, thyme, and salt. Simmer until the potatoes are tender.

Makes 4 servings

One serving = 192 calories
            11 g protein
            16 g carbohydrate
            4 g fat
            482 mg sodium

One serving = 1 low-fat protein + 1 starch/bread + ½ milk + 1 vegetable

Broccoli Cheese Soup

1 pound fresh or frozen broccoli
3 cups water
2 yellow onions, sliced thin
1½ tablespoons all-purpose flour
½ teaspoon salt
2 cups low-fat milk
½ cup grated cheddar cheese

Cook the broccoli in the water with the onions until broccoli is tender. Cool and puree in a blender or food processor. Return the puree to the pan. Combine the flour, salt, and milk in a bowl. Stir the flour mixture into the pureed broccoli and simmer over medium heat until thickened, about 15 minutes. Add the cheese and stir until melted. Remove from the heat and serve.

Makes 4 servings

One serving = 241 calories
11 g protein
22 g carbohydrate
12 g fat
464 mg sodium

One serving = 1 starch/bread + 1 vegetable + 1 high-fat protein

Mulligatawny Soup

This is a tasty soup that originated in India. *Mulligatawny* means "pepper water," referring to the effect of the curry powder. It can be served hot or cold.

> 6 cups chicken broth
> 1 cup diced cooked chicken
> 1 yellow onion, chopped
> 1 apple, cored and chopped
> 1 green bell pepper, chopped
> 2 carrots, sliced
> 2 ribs celery, chopped
> 1 teaspoon salt
> 2-4 teaspoons curry powder
> ⅛ teaspoon ground nutmeg
> 2 cups cooked white or brown
>   rice

Combine all the ingredients in a large saucepan. Cook, uncovered, over medium heat for 30–40 minutes or until the vegetables are tender.

Makes 8 servings

One serving = 195 calories
              13 g protein
              24 g carbohydrate
              4 g fat
              427 mg sodium

One serving = 2 low-fat protein + 1 starch/bread + 1 vegetable

M i n e s t r o n e

1 yellow onion, chopped
1 clove garlic, minced
1 teaspoon dried oregano leaves
1 teaspoon dried basil leaves
1 tablespoon dried parsley leaves
1 cup chopped celery
1 cup sliced carrot
2 cups sliced zucchini
2 28-ounce cans whole tomatoes
*   with the juice*
1 16-ounce can white
*   (cannellini) or red kidney*
*   beans*
6 cups water
1 cup elbow macaroni

Combine all the ingredients in a large saucepan or Dutch oven. Cover and simmer for 2–3 hours, until the macaroni is cooked and the vegetables are tender.

Makes 12 servings

One serving = 122 calories
              8 g protein
              16 g carbohydrate
              1 g fat
              333 mg sodium

One serving = 1 starch/bread + 1 low-fat protein + 1 vegetable

Fresh Fruit Gazpacho

3 large fresh tomatoes, peeled
    and seeded (see note)
3 cups orange juice
1 tablespoon sugar
1 cantaloupe, peeled, seeded,
    and cubed
1 honeydew melon, peeled,
    seeded, and cubed
1 papaya, peeled, seeded, and
    cubed
1 cup fresh strawberries, sliced
1 kiwifruit, peeled and sliced
    thin
Ground cardamom for garnish

Combine the tomatoes, 1 cup of the orange juice, the sugar, and about half the cantaloupe cubes in a food processor. Process until smooth. Pour into a serving bowl. Repeat with 1 cup orange juice, the rest of the cantaloupe, and some of the honeydew. Process until smooth. Pour into the serving bowl. Puree the rest of the honeydew and the papaya in the last cup of orange juice. Add to the serving bowl. Stir. Place the strawberry and kiwifruit slices in the fruit puree. Refrigerate until cold, at least 3 to 4 hours. Sprinkle on the cardamom just before serving.

Makes 8 servings

Note: To peel and seed tomatoes, bring a pot of water to a
boil, drop in the tomatoes, and boil for about 10 seconds.
Remove the tomatoes with a slotted spoon and slip off the
skins. Core the tomatoes, cut them into quarters, and
squeeze gently to squeeze out the juice and seeds.
One serving = 106 calories

        0 g protein
       23 g carbohydrate
        0 g fat
     11 mg sodium

One serving = 2 fruit

Red Cabbage and Apple Soup

1 small head red cabbage
3 scallions, chopped fine
1 clove garlic, minced
1 tablespoon margarine or butter
1 cup tomato or V-8 juice
1 apple, peeled, cored, and
    chopped
1 potato, peeled and diced
3 cups chicken broth
Chopped chives for garnish

Shred the cabbage. In a large saucepan, sauté the scallions and garlic in the margarine for about 2–3 minutes, until tender and translucent. Add the tomato juice, shredded cabbage, apple, potato, and chicken broth. Bring to a boil, then reduce the heat and simmer, covered for 30 minutes. Puree the soup in a blender or food processor. Return it to the pot to reheat, then sprinkle with chopped chives and serve.

Makes 4 servings

One serving = 41 calories
          2 g protein
          9 g carbohydrate
          2 g fat
          182 mg sodium

One serving = 2 vegetable

MAIN DISHES

Mexican Flank Steak

4 dried hot red peppers
2 tablespoons hot water
2 cloves garlic
2 tablespoons wine vinegar
½ teaspoon ground cumin
1½ pounds beef flank steak
1 14-ounce can whole tomatoes,
    drained, or 6 fresh tomatoes,
    peeled and seeded (see
    Index)

Soak the hot peppers in the hot water for 15 minutes. Pour off the water and remove the seeds from the peppers. Combine the garlic, vinegar, pepper skins, and cumin in a food processor. Process until smooth. Spread the vegetable paste over one side of the flank steak. Cover and refrigerate overnight or for at least 4 hours.

Preheat the oven to 350°F. Place the steak in a roasting pan and add the tomatoes. Cover and bake for 40–50 minutes. Uncover and bake for 10 minutes longer. Cut the steak into thin slices to serve.

Makes 6 servings

Note: Whenever you handle fresh or dried hot peppers, be sure to wear rubber gloves and avoid touching your face.

One serving = 227 calories
          27 g protein
          7 g carbohydrate
          10 g fat
          266 mg sodium

One serving = 3 low-fat protein + 1 vegetable

Bankruptcy Stew

2 pounds boneless lean beef
    round steak
½ cup water
½ cup tomato sauce
4 large potatoes, peeled and
    cubed
1 green bell pepper, sliced thin
1 rib celery, chopped
1 yellow onion, sliced thin
3 carrots, peeled and sliced
1 sprig fresh parsley or 1
    tablespoon dried parsley
    leaves
1 bay leaf

Cut the round steak into 1-inch cubes. Brown the beef cubes over high heat in a nonstick skillet. Add the rest of the ingredients to the skillet. Cover and simmer for 1 hour over medium heat until the meat is tender.

Makes 8 servings

One serving = 345 calories
            23 g protein
            22 g carbohydrate
            12 g fat
            482 mg sodium

One serving = 3 low-fat protein + 1 starch/bread + 1 vegetable

Taco Pie

1 12-ounce bag corn chips
1 pound ground beef
½ cup minced onion
1 clove garlic, minced
½ cup bottled taco sauce
½ cup canned refried beans
2 cups chopped lettuce
½ cup chopped green bell pepper
¼ cup chopped scallion
1 tomato, chopped fine
¼ pound Monterey Jack or
    cheddar cheese
Salsa for serving

Spread the corn chips in the bottom of a 13″ × 9″ pan. In a nonstick skillet, sauté the ground beef with the onion, garlic, and taco sauce over medium heat for about 3–5 minutes, until the onions are tender. Stir in the refried beans. Spread the meat mixture over the corn chips. Sprinkle the lettuce, green pepper, scallions, and tomato over the meat mixture. Top with cheese and serve with salsa.

Makes 6 servings

One serving = 481 calories
            29 g protein
            32 g carbohydrate
            21 g fat
            684 mg sodium

One serving = 3 medium-fat protein + 2 vegetable + 2 starch/bread + 2 fat

Impossible Taco Pie

1 pound lean ground beef
½ cup chopped yellow onion
1 envelope taco seasoning mix
2 cups all-purpose flour
2 teaspoons baking powder
¾ cup skim milk
1 large egg
⅓ cup vegetable oil
¼ pound Monterey Jack or
  cheddar cheese, grated (1 cup)
½ cup chopped tomatoes
Shredded lettuce, chopped fresh
  chilies, and chopped ripe
  olives for serving

Preheat the oven to 400°F. Brown the ground beef and onions in nonstick skillet. Drain off any fat. Stir in the taco seasoning mix. Spread the beef mixture in the bottom of a lightly oiled 2-quart casserole dish. Combine the flour, baking powder, milk, egg, and oil in a bowl. Beat with a wire whip until blended. Pour the flour mixture over the beef mixture. Sprinkle on the cheese and tomatoes. Bake for 30–40 minutes or until the crust is done.

Makes 6 servings

One serving = 397 calories
          25 g protein
          18 g carbohydrate
          27 g fat
          481 mg sodium

One serving = 3 medium-fat protein + 1 starch/bread + 2 fat + 1 vegetable

Pork Chops
in Orange Ginger Sauce

4 pork chops
1 yellow onion, sliced thin
½ cup orange juice
2 teaspoons honey
½ teaspoon ground ginger
Orange slices for garnish

Brown the pork chops on both sides with the onions in a nonstick skillet over medium-high heat. Add the juice, honey, and ginger. Cover and cook over medium heat for 45–50 minutes or until the pork chops are tender. Garnish with orange slices.

Makes 4 servings

One serving = 214 calories
20 g protein
5 g carbohydrate
13 g fat
181 mg sodium

One serving = 3 medium-fat protein

Cinnamon Apple
Pork Tenderloin

1 pound pork tenderloin
2 tablespoons cornstarch
1 teaspoon ground cinnamon
2 apples, peeled, cored, and
*   sliced*
2 tablespoons raisins

Preheat the oven to 400°F. Place the pork tenderloin in a roasting pan or casserole dish with a lid. Combine the rest of the ingredients in a bowl and toss to blend. Spoon the apple mixture around the pork tenderloin, cover, and bake for 40 minutes. Remove the lid and spoon the apple mixture over the tenderloin. Return it to the oven and bake for 15–20 minutes longer, until the tenderloin is browned and cooked through.

Makes 4 servings

One serving = 267 calories
             20 g protein
             13 g carbohydrate
             10 g fat
             148 mg sodium

One serving = 3 medium-fat protein + 1 fruit

Ham Steak with Mustard Pineapple Sauce

1 pound ham steak
¼ cup plain low-fat yogurt
1 teaspoon prepared mustard
1 teaspoon dried tarragon leaves
½ cup canned pineapple chunks
      in their own juice

Preheat the broiler. Place the ham steak on a baking sheet and broil 3 inches from the heat for 10 minutes or until heated through. Combine the yogurt, mustard, and tarragon. Top the ham slice with yogurt sauce. Place the pineapple chunks on top of the ham and broil for 2–3 minutes longer or until browned.

Makes 4 servings

One serving = 265 calories
            23 g protein
            7 g carbohydrate
            12 g fat
            721 mg sodium

One serving = 3 medium-fat protein + ½ fruit

Baked Chicken Parmesan

1 3-pound chicken, cut up
½ cup wheat germ
1 tablespoon freshly grated
    Parmesan cheese
1 teaspoon Italian seasoning
1 tablespoon dried parsley flakes

Preheat the oven to 350°F. Rinse the chicken with cold water. Prepare the coating mixture by combining the rest of the ingredients. Shake off excess water from the chicken and coat all sides with the wheat germ mixture. Place the chicken in a shallow baking dish and bake for 40–50 minutes, until cooked through.

To cook in a microwave, arrange the chicken pieces on a microwave-safe plate with the thicker pieces toward the outside of the dish. Cover with a glass lid. Microwave on HIGH for 12–15 minutes or until the thickest parts are no longer pink.

Makes 4 servings

One serving = 255 calories
            22 g protein
            10 g carbohydrate
            4 g fat
            117 mg sodium

One serving = 3 low-fat protein + ½ starch/bread

Chicken Legs and Sweet Potatoes

4 chicken legs and thighs
1 tablespoon olive oil
¼ cup chopped yellow onion
4 large shallots, peeled and
    sliced
8 medium-size fresh mushrooms,
    sliced
4 (about 1 pound) sweet
    potatoes, peeled and halved
    lengthwise
1 cup apple juice
8 large cloves garlic, peeled and
    minced
½ teaspoon salt
¼ teaspoon ground white pepper
Chopped fresh parsley for
    garnish

Skin the chicken. Heat the olive oil over medium-high heat in a large skillet and brown the chicken pieces on all sides for about 10 minutes. Add the rest of the ingredients except the parsley and bring to a boil. Cover and reduce the heat to medium. Cook for 30 minutes or until the chicken is cooked through. Garnish with parsley before serving.

Makes 4 servings

One serving = 193 calories
            25 g protein
            18 g carbohydrate
            10 g fat
            266 mg sodium

One serving = 3 low-fat protein + 1 starch/bread

Chicken Cassoulet

1 teaspoon olive oil
½ cup chopped scallion or
    shallot
1 clove garlic, minced
1 pound boneless, skinless
    chicken breasts, cut into
    bite-size pieces
1 teaspoon dried thyme leaves
1 teaspoon ground coriander
½ teaspoon salt
1 28-ounce can whole tomatoes,
    chopped, with the juice
1 19-ounce can cannellini (white
    kidney beans), drained

Preheat the oven to 350°F. Heat the oil in a large skillet over medium heat. Add the scallions and garlic and sauté for about 2 minutes, until onions are tender. Add the remaining ingredients and bring to a boil. Pour the mixture into a 3-quart casserole, cover, and bake for 30–40 minutes or until the chicken is cooked through.

Makes 6 servings

One serving = 252 calories
           27 g protein
           24 g carbohydrate
           8 g fat
           365 mg sodium

One serving = 3 low-fat protein + 1 starch/bread + 1 vegetable

B r u n s w i c k   S t e w

1 (about 6 pounds) stewing hen,
    cut up
2–3 quarts water
2 large yellow onions, sliced
2 cups okra slices
4 cups chopped fresh tomatoes
2 cups frozen lima beans
3 medium-size potatoes, diced
4 cups fresh or frozen corn kernels
2 teaspoons salt
1 teaspoon freshly ground pepper

Put the hen and water—3 quarts for a thin stew, 2 quarts for a thick stew—into a Dutch oven or heavy stockpot. Simmer, covered, skimming foam off the surface as necessary, until the meat pulls easily away from the bones, about 2 hours. Remove the chicken and set it aside to cool.

Add the onions, okra, tomatoes, lima beans, potatoes, and corn to the broth. Simmer, uncovered, stirring occasionally to prevent scorching, until the beans and potatoes are tender, about 45 minutes.

Remove the chicken meat from the bones and dice. Add the diced chicken, salt, and pepper to the stew. Heat through before serving.

Makes 8 servings

One serving = 305 calories
            17 g protein
            37 g carbohydrate
            8 g fat
            418 mg sodium

One serving = 2 low-fat protein + 2 starch/bread + 1 vegetable

Cornish Hens with Raspberry Sauce

3 Cornish hens
1 10-ounce box frozen red
raspberries in light syrup,
thawed
1 teaspoon cornstarch

Preheat the oven to 350°F. Wash and drain the Cornish hens. Cut them in half and place the halves in a roasting pan, breast side up. Roast for 1 hour or until cooked through.

While the hens are roasting, place the raspberries in a blender and blend until smooth. Then push the puree through a sieve to remove the seeds if desired. Combine the raspberry puree and cornstarch in a saucepan. Mix well. Cook the raspberry mixture over medium heat until slightly thickened and hot. Cover and keep warm until ready to serve. Serve the sauce hot on top of the Cornish hens.

Makes 6 servings

One serving = 149 calories
20 g protein
8 g carbohydrate
4 g fat
59 mg sodium

One serving = 3 low-fat protein + ½ fruit

Cornish Hens with Apple Stuffing

2 Cornish hens
1 small yellow onion, chopped
1 apple, peeled, cored, and
　　chopped
1 rib celery, chopped
4 slices bread, cubed
2 teaspoons margarine or butter,
　　melted
½ teaspoon dried sage leaves
½ teaspoon dried thyme leaves
⅛ teaspoon ground pepper

Preheat the oven to 350°F. Rinse the Cornish hens and open each cavity for the stuffing. Combine the rest of the ingredients in a bowl. Toss to mix. Fill the Cornish hen cavities with the stuffing. Place the hens breast side up in a shallow baking pan and roast for 40–50 minutes or until the hens are tender.

Makes 4 servings

One serving = 189 calories
　　　　　　　22 g protein
　　　　　　　24 g carbohydrate
　　　　　　　7 g fat
　　　　　　　199 mg sodium

One serving = 3 low-fat protein + 1 starch/bread + ½ fruit

Turkey Quiche

2 cups chopped cooked turkey
1 cup sliced fresh mushrooms
½ cup chopped scallion
*2 ounces Swiss cheese, grated (½
  cup)*
1 cup skim milk
2 cups all-purpose flour
2 teaspoons baking powder
1 large egg
⅓ cup vegetable oil

Preheat the oven to 400°F. Combine the turkey, mushrooms, scallions, and cheese in a bowl. Stir to mix. Spread in the bottom of an oiled 2-quart casserole. Beat together the milk, flour, baking powder, egg, and oil. Pour over the turkey mixture. Bake for 40–45 minutes, until knife inserted into center comes out clean.

Makes 6 servings

One serving = 271 calories
              23 g protein
              19 g carbohydrate
              16 g fat
              207 mg sodium

One serving = 3 low-fat protein + 1 starch/bread + 1 fat

Turkey-Sausage Sandwich

1 pound ground turkey
1 teaspoon dried ground sage
1 teaspoon fennel seeds
½ cup unsweetened apple butter
8 English muffins, split and
toasted

Combine the ground turkey, sage, and fennel seeds in a bowl. Mix well. Refrigerate overnight for best flavor. Shape the turkey mixture into eight patties. Flatten and cook in a nonstick skillet over medium heat for about 10 minutes. Turn and cook about 3 minutes more. Spread the apple butter on the English muffin halves. Top each with a ground turkey patty. Place the other English muffin half over each patty to make a sandwich

Makes 8 servings

One serving = 269 calories
             16 g protein
             36 g carbohydrate
             5 g fat
             362 mg sodium

One serving = 2 starch/bread + 2 low-fat protein

Greek Meatballs

1 pound ground turkey
¼ cup plain low-fat yogurt
½ cup chopped scallion
1 clove garlic, minced
1 fresh tomato, peeled, seeded
(see Index), and chopped
fine
2 tablespoons freshly grated
Parmesan cheese
½ teaspoon salt
¼ cup dried bread crumbs
2 tablespoons chopped cilantro
or fresh parsley or 1
tablespoon dried parsley
1 teaspoon dried oregano leaves

Preheat the oven to 350°F. Combine all the ingredients in a bowl and mix well. Shape into 1-inch meatballs and place in a baking pan. Bake for 25–30 minutes or until the meatballs are cooked through. Place the meatballs and juice in a chafing dish over a low flame to serve. Use six meatballs per main-dish serving or two meatballs per snack or appetizer serving.

Makes 24 meatballs

One serving of 6 meatballs = 195 calories
24 g protein
15 g carbohydrate
12 g fat
363 mg sodium

One serving = 3 low-fat protein + 1 starch/bread

Deep-Dish Pizza

1 pound ground turkey
2 cups all-purpose flour
2 teaspoons baking powder
½ teaspoon baking soda
¼ cup margarine or butter
½–¾ cup skim milk
1 6-ounce can tomato paste
1 teaspoon dried oregano leaves
½ teaspoon dried basil leaves
½ teaspoon dried thyme leaves
½ teaspoon salt
½ cup chopped green bell pepper
½ cup sliced fresh mushrooms
¼ pound mozzarella cheese,
        grated (1 cup)

Preheat the oven to 425°F. Cook the ground turkey in a large nonstick skillet over medium heat until cooked through, stirring occasionally. Meanwhile, combine the flour, baking powder, baking soda, and margarine in a bowl. Cut the margarine into the flour with a fork or pastry blender until the mixture resembles coarse meal. Add enough milk to make a soft, elastic dough, like biscuit dough. Press the dough into the sides and bottom of an 8-inch square baking pan. Combine the tomato paste, oregano, basil, thyme, and salt and spread over the dough. Crumble the ground turkey over the sauce. Sprinkle on the green pepper, mushrooms, and cheese. Bake for 20–25 minutes or until the crust is brown and crisp. Cut into four squares to serve.

Makes 4 servings

One serving = 358 calories
               26 g protein
               34 g carbohydrate
               20 g fat
               584 mg sodium

One serving = 3 low-fat protein + 1 starch/bread + 2 vegetable + 2 fat

Creole Flounder

1 small green bell pepper, cut
    into thin strips
½ cup sliced scallion
1 tablespoon olive oil
1 14½-ounce can whole
    tomatoes, chopped, with
    the juice
1 8-ounce can tomato sauce
1 teaspoon dried thyme leaves
1 bay leaf
1 pound flounder fillets

Preheat the oven to 375°F. In a skillet over medium heat, sauté the green pepper and scallions in the olive oil until tender, about 5 minutes. Stir in the tomatoes, tomato sauce, thyme, and bay leaf. Simmer for 15–20 minutes to blend the flavors. Place the flounder fillets in a lightly oiled baking pan and spoon the sauce over them. Bake for 15–20 minutes or until the fish flakes with a fork.

Makes 4 servings

One serving = 168 calories
             22 g protein
             8 g carbohydrate
             4 g fat
             319 mg sodium

One serving = 3 low-fat protein + 1 vegetable

Fish Fillets with Grapefruit

1 pound sole, cod, snapper, or
orange roughy fillets
½ cup fresh grapefruit juice
2 teaspoons ground coriander
1 pink grapefruit, sectioned

Preheat the oven to 400°F. Place the fish fillets in a shallow pan and pour the grapefruit juice over them. Sprinkle on the coriander and marinate in the refrigerator for 30–60 minutes. Bake for 10–15 minutes or until the fish flakes with a fork. Serve with the grapefruit sections.

Makes 4 servings

One serving = 89 calories
20 g protein
1 g carbohydrate
2 g fat
57 mg sodium

One serving = 3 low-fat protein

New England Halibut Stew

2 carrots, sliced
2 ribs celery, chopped
½ cup chopped yellow onion
2 cloves garlic, minced
1 tablespoon olive oil
1 28-ounce can whole tomatoes,
    with the juice
½ cup water
3 tablespoons minced fresh
    parsley
½ teaspoon dried thyme leaves
½ teaspoon dried basil leaves
⅛ teaspoon freshly ground white
    pepper
1 pound halibut or salmon fillets

Sauté the carrots, celery, onion, and garlic in the oil in a skillet over medium heat for 5 minutes. Add the rest of the ingredients, except the fish, breaking up the tomatoes with a spoon. Cover and simmer for 20 minutes. Cut the fish into 1-inch cubes and add to the stew. Cover and simmer for 5–10 minutes or until the halibut flakes when tested with a fork.

Makes 4 servings

One serving = 171 calories
            24 g protein
            12 g carbohydrate
            5 g fat
            208 mg sodium

One serving = 3 low-fat protein + 2 vegetable

Broiled Macadamia Tuna Delight

2 8-ounce tuna steaks
½ cup juice-packed crushed
    pineapple
2 tablespoons chopped scallion
1 teaspoon minced jalapeño or
    other fresh hot pepper
    (optional)
¼ cup finely chopped
    macadamia nuts

Preheat the broiler. Place the tuna steaks on a broiler pan. Combine the pineapple, scallions, and jalapeño. Spoon over the tuna steaks. Broil 4 inches from the heat until the tuna flakes with a fork, about 5 minutes. Remove from the oven and sprinkle on the nuts. Broil for 1–2 minutes more, just until the nuts are toasted. Serve immediately.

Makes 4 servings

One serving = 191 calories
            23 g protein
            7 g carbohydrate
            10 g fat
            67 mg sodium

One serving = 3 low-fat protein + 1 fat

Tuna   Rice   Casserole

1 6½-ounce can water-packed
    tuna, drained and flaked
1 cup cooked white or brown
    rice
½ cup chopped fresh
    mushrooms
¼ cup chopped celery
¼ cup chopped fresh tomato
¼ cup chopped green bell pepper
¼ teaspoon dried basil leaves
¼ teaspoon dried dill weed
1 tablespoon mayonnaise

Preheat the oven to 375°F. Combine all the ingredients in a bowl, then transfer the mixture to a lightly oiled 2-quart baking dish. Bake, uncovered, until browned, about 20 minutes.

Makes 2 servings

One serving = 275 calories
               22 g protein
               18 g carbohydrate
               8 g fat
               351 mg sodium

One serving = 3 low-fat protein + 1 starch/bread + 1 fat + 1 vegetable

Seafood Scampi

2 tablespoons olive oil
2 cloves garlic, minced
1 fresh tomato, peeled, seeded
    (see Index), and chopped fine
2 tablespoons fresh lemon juice
2 tablespoons chopped fresh
    parsley
1/4 teaspoon dried oregano
1/8 teaspoon freshly ground black
    pepper
1/2 pound shrimp, peeled
1/2 pound bay or sea scallops
1 dozen mussels or clams

Combine all the ingredients except seafood in a microwave-safe bowl. Cover and microwave on HIGH for 3 minutes. Place the seafood in another microwave-safe casserole or dish. Pour the tomato mixture over the seafood. Microwave on HIGH for 3–5 minutes or until the shrimp is tender and the mussels have opened.

To cook on the stove and in a conventional oven, preheat the oven to 350°F. Cook the sauce ingredients in a saucepan over medium heat for 10 minutes. Pour the sauce over the seafood in a casserole dish and bake for 15–20 minutes or until the mussels have opened.

Makes 4 servings

One serving = 148 calories
            20 g protein
            4 g carbohydrate
            6 g fat
            99 mg sodium

One serving = 3 low-fat protein

Florida Herbed Scallops

1 pound bay or sea scallops
1 tablespoon olive oil
½ cup fresh grapefruit juice
2 tablespoons chopped fresh
   parsley
1 clove garlic, minced
1 teaspoon dried tarragon leaves
½ cup toasted fresh bread
   crumbs

Cut the scallops into bite-size pieces if sea scallops are used. Combine the olive oil, juice, parsley, garlic, and tarragon in a skillet. Bring to a boil, add the scallops, and reduce the heat to medium. Poach until the scallops are tender—3–5 minutes. Top with the bread crumbs just before serving.

Makes 4 servings

One serving = 135 calories
            23 g protein
            4 g carbohydrate
            3 g fat
            71 mg sodium

One serving = 3 low-fat protein

Shrimp Creole

½ cup chopped celery
½ cup chopped yellow onion
1 clove garlic, minced
½ cup (2 ounces) diced lean
    ham
1 28-ounce can whole tomatoes,
    with the juice
1 8-ounce can tomato sauce
½ teaspoon chili powder
½ teaspoon ground thyme
1 pound peeled, cooked shrimp
Tabasco sauce to taste

Sauté the celery, onion, garlic, and ham in a nonstick skillet over medium heat until the celery is tender, about 5 minutes. Add the rest of the ingredients and cook, uncovered, for 20 minutes over medium heat. Serve over rice.

Makes 6 servings

One serving = 190 calories
              22 g protein
              5 g carbohydrate
              6 g fat
              318 mg sodium

One serving = 3 low-fat protein + 1 vegetable

Shrimp Curry

1 teaspoon margarine or butter
1 small yellow onion, chopped
¼ cup chopped green bell pepper
1 clove garlic, minced
¾ teaspoon curry powder
½ teaspoon chili powder
¼ teaspoon ground ginger
½ cup plain yogurt
¾ pound cooked, peeled, and
    deveined medium-size
    shrimp (1¼ pounds
    uncooked shrimp in shells)

In a nonstick saucepan, melt the margarine. Add and sauté the onion, green pepper, garlic, and spices over medium heat for 3–4 minutes. Add the yogurt and shrimp. Cover and cook over low heat until hot, stirring occasionally. Serve over a bed of rice.

Makes 4 servings

One serving = 147 calories
             23 g protein
             7 g carbohydrate
             5 g fat
             187 mg sodium

One serving = 3 low-fat protein

Lobster Newburg

1 pound lobster tail, cooked
½ pound small shrimp, cooked
1 tablespoon margarine or butter
1 tablespoon all-purpose flour
½ teaspoon salt
⅛ teaspoon paprika
Pinch cayenne pepper
½ cup low-fat milk
¼ cup dry white wine

Cut the lobster meat into ½-inch pieces. Shell the shrimp. Melt the margarine in a skillet. Add the flour, salt, paprika, and cayenne. Cook over medium heat 2 minutes. Stir in the milk to make a thick sauce. Pour in the wine and stir until the sauce is smooth. Add the lobster and shrimp and heat for 2–3 minutes. Serve over rice or noodles.

Makes 2 servings

One serving = 257 calories
31 g protein
7 g carbohydrate
9 g fat
692 mg sodium

One serving = 4 low-fat protein

Hearty Vegetarian Chili

1 15½-ounce can Great Northern
     beans, drained
1 15½-ounce can red kidney
     beans, drained
1 15½-ounce can chick-peas
     (garbanzo beans), drained
1 16-ounce can whole tomatoes,
     with the juice
1 6-ounce can tomato paste
½ cup chopped yellow onion
1 small clove garlic, minced
1–2 teaspoons chili powder
Chopped onion, chopped green
     bell pepper, and/or grated
     cheese for garnish

Combine all the ingredients in a saucepan or slow cooker. Heat over medium heat for 30 minutes to blend the flavors or heat on low heat in a slow cooker for 3–4 hours. Garnish as desired.

Makes 7 cups

One serving of 1½ cups = 273 calories
                        21 g protein
                        41 g carbohydrate
                        4 g fat
                        617 mg sodium

One serving = 2 starch/bread + 2 low-fat protein + 1 vegetable

Bean Burgers

1 16-ounce can pinto beans
1½ cups dried bread crumbs
2 tablespoons barbecue sauce
¼ teaspoon salt
1 tablespoon vegetable oil
6 slices (6 ounces) American
    cheese
6 hamburger buns

Mash the beans and liquid with a potato masher or in a blender. Add the bread crumbs, barbecue sauce, and salt. Mix well and shape into six patties. Heat the oil in a skillet and fry the patties over medium heat until well browned on both sides. Top each burger with a slice of cheese. Serve on buns with additional barbecue sauce and onion if desired.

Makes 6 servings

One serving = 487 calories
            26 g protein
            47 g carbohydrate
            7 g fat
            681 mg sodium

One serving = 3 starch/bread + 3 low-fat protein

Black Beans on Rice

*¼ pound (½ cup) dried black
    beans*
2 cups boiling water
1 green bell pepper, chopped
1 small yellow onion, chopped
½ clove garlic
1-2 tablespoons vegetable oil
½ teaspoon salt
¼ pound (1 cup) brown rice
2 cups water
*Grated cheese for garnish
    (optional)*

Cover the beans with the boiling water and cook for 1 hour. In a small skillet over medium heat, sauté the green pepper, onions, and garlic in the oil. Combine with beans; add the salt and cook until the beans are tender and the liquid is thick, about 1 hour. Meanwhile, cook the brown rice in the water as directed on the package, for 40–45 minutes or until tender. Serve the beans over the rice, with grated cheese sprinkled on top if desired.

Makes 4 servings

One serving = 248 calories
               12 g protein
               13 g carbohydrate
               5 g fat
               387 mg sodium

One serving = 2 starch/bread + 2 low-fat protein

L e n t i l   S p a g h e t t i   S a u c e

1 cup lentils
2 16-ounce cans whole tomatoes,
*   with the juice*
2 cloves garlic, minced
½ pound fresh mushrooms,
*   sliced*
1 yellow onion, chopped
1 cup water
1 teaspoon dried oregano leaves
½ teaspoon dried parsley leaves
⅛ teaspoon ground nutmeg
1 teaspoon salt
2 tablespoons freshly grated
*   Parmesan cheese (optional)*

Combine all the ingredients except Parmesan cheese in a large saucepan or slow cooker. Simmer over low heat for 1 hour on the stove or 4 hours in the slow cooker, until the lentils are soft. Serve over cooked spaghetti. Sprinkle with grated Parmesan cheese before serving.

Makes 4 servings

One serving = 193 calories
            16 g protein
            24 g carbohydrate
            4 g fat
            497 mg sodium

One serving = 1 starch/bread + 2 low-fat protein + 1 vegetable

Vegetable Spaghetti Sauce

1 yellow onion
1 clove garlic, minced
1 teaspoon olive oil
1 cup chopped celery
1 cup chopped green bell pepper
2 cups cubed zucchini
1 cup sliced carrot
2 8-ounce cans tomato sauce
1 6-ounce can tomato paste
2 cups water
1 teaspoon dried thyme leaves
½ teaspoon dried oregano leaves

In a large saucepan, brown the onion and garlic in the oil over medium heat for about 5 minutes. Add the rest of the ingredients and simmer over medium heat for at least 1 hour to cook the vegetables. Serve over cooked spaghetti.

Makes 6 servings

One serving = 37 calories
              3 g protein
              12 g carbohydrate
              1 g fat
              211 mg sodium

One serving = 2 vegetable

Cheesy Vegetable Loaf

3 cups cooked lentils
½ cup chopped yellow onion
*1 cup chopped fresh spinach or
  kale*
1 cup grated carrot
2 tablespoons olive oil
½ teaspoon dried sage
1 teaspoon salt
½ teaspoon celery seeds
*½ cup oatmeal or dried whole-
  wheat bread crumbs*
*½ cup grated cheddar or Swiss
  cheese (optional)*

Preheat the oven to 350°F. Combine all the ingredients except cheese in a mixing bowl. Stir to mix thoroughly. Spoon into a lightly oiled 2-quart casserole or loaf pan. Sprinkle on the grated cheese if desired. Bake for 50–60 minutes, until browned on top.

Makes 6 servings

One serving (includes cheese) = 293 calories
                              16 g protein
                              24 g carbohydrate
                              7 g fat
                              584 mg sodium

One serving = 2 starch/bread + 2 low-fat protein + 1 vegetable + 1 fat

Spinach Rice Casserole

1 tablespoon olive oil
1 large yellow onion, chopped
2 cups sliced fresh mushrooms
1 clove garlic, minced
1 large egg
1 tablespoon whole-wheat flour
2 cups low-fat cottage cheese
10 ounces frozen chopped
*   spinach, defrosted and*
*   drained, or 1 pound fresh spinach*
3 cups cooked brown rice
½ teaspoon dried thyme leaves
2 tablespoons freshly grated
*   Parmesan cheese*
2 tablespoons sunflower seeds

Preheat the oven to 375°F. Heat the oil in a Dutch oven and sauté the onions, mushrooms, and garlic over medium heat for about 5 minutes, until tender. In a small bowl, mix the egg, flour, and cottage cheese. Add to the sautéed vegetables along with the spinach. Stir in the rice, thyme, and 1 tablespoon of the Parmesan cheese. Transfer the mixture to a greased 12″ × 8″ baking dish and top with the remaining Parmesan cheese and the sunflower seeds. Bake for 30 minutes.

Makes 6 servings

One serving = 258 calories
              14 g protein
              19 g carbohydrate
              8 g fat
              289 mg sodium

One serving = 2 low-fat protein + 1 starch/bread + 2 vegetable + 1 fat

Pineapple Cheddar Rice

½ cup brown rice
1 cup water
1 8-ounce can juice-packed
    crushed pineapple
½ cup grated cheddar cheese
½ cup frozen peas, defrosted
¼ cup chopped celery
¼ cup chopped scallion
¼ cup chopped red or green bell
    pepper
¼ teaspoon dried tarragon
    leaves
1 small garlic clove, minced

Cook the rice in 1 cup water in a saucepan according to the directions on the package, until tender. Stir in the rest of the ingredients and simmer for 10 minutes to blend the flavors. Serve warm.

Makes 4 servings

One serving = 227 calories
            11 g protein
            28 g carbohydrate
            10 g fat
            216 mg sodium

One serving = 1 starch/bread + 1 medium-fat protein + 1 fruit

Spinach   Barley   Casserole

1 cup quick-cooking barley
2 cups water
1 10-ounce package frozen
    chopped spinach, defrosted
    and well drained
1 cup chopped fresh mushrooms
½ cup chopped yellow onion
1 clove garlic, minced
½ cup crumbled feta cheese
1 cup part-skim ricotta or low-
    fat cottage cheese
1 cup plain low-fat yogurt
4 large eggs
½ teaspoon dried dill weed
¼ teaspoon ground nutmeg
¼ teaspoon salt
⅛ teaspoon freshly ground white
    pepper

Cook the barley in the water according to the package directions. Remove from the heat and let stand for 5 minutes. Set aside. Preheat the oven to 350°F. Spray an 11″ × 7″ baking dish with nonstick cooking spray or oil lightly.

Cook the spinach, mushrooms, onion, and garlic in a nonstick skillet over low heat for 4–5 minutes or until the onion is tender. Remove from the heat and set aside. In a large bowl, combine the cheeses, yogurt, eggs, dill weed, nutmeg, salt, and pepper. Mix well. Stir in the barley and spinach mixture. Spread into the prepared dish and bake for 40–45 minutes or until the edges are set and a knife inserted in the center comes out clean. Let stand for 15 minutes. Serve warm.

Makes 8 servings

One serving = 226 calories
15 g protein
21 g carbohydrate
5 g fat
227 mg sodium

One serving = 2 medium-fat protein + 1 starch/bread + 1 vegetable

Vegetarian Lasagna

10 ounces lasagna noodles
1 pound part-skim ricotta or
 low-fat cottage cheese
1½ cups chopped cooked fresh
 spinach or 1 10-ounce
 package frozen chopped
 spinach, defrosted and
 squeezed to drain well
1 cup spaghetti sauce, bottled
1½ cups (½ pound) grated
 mozzarella cheese
¼ cup freshly grated Parmesan
 cheese

Preheat the oven to 350°F. Cook the lasagna noodles until just tender according to the package directions. Blend the ricotta cheese and spinach together. Line a lightly oiled 13″ × 9″ baking pan with one-third of the noodles. Spoon half the ricotta mixture over the noodles. Pour on ½ cup of the sauce. Sprinkle on ½ cup of the mozzarella and 2 tablespoons of the Parmesan. Repeat the layering with one-third of the noodles, the rest of the ricotta mixture, ½ cup of the mozzarella, and 1 tablespoon of the Parmesan. Place the remaining third of the noodles on top. Spread the remaining sauce over the top and then sprinkle on the rest of the cheeses. Bake for 35–40 minutes, until cooked through.

Makes 8 servings

One serving = 389 calories
22 g protein
26 g carbohydrate
18 g fat
719 mg sodium

One serving = 1 starch/bread + 3 medium-fat protein + 2 vegetable

Zesty Chef's Salad

1 cup chopped romaine lettuce
1 ounce part-skim mozzarella
    cheese, cubed
1 ounce lean ham, cubed
1 ounce cooked turkey breast,
    cubed

DRESSING

$\frac{1}{4}$ cup vegetable or olive oil
$\frac{1}{4}$ cup water
1 teaspoon minced onion
1 clove garlic, minced
$\frac{1}{4}$ teaspoon paprika
$\frac{3}{4}$ cup fresh grapefruit juice

Arrange the lettuce on a plate and top with the cheese, ham, and turkey cubes. Make the dressing by combining the ingredients in a jar. Shake well and pour 2 tablespoons over the salad ingredients.

Makes 1 serving of salad and 12 servings (1$\frac{1}{2}$ cups) of dressing.

One serving of 2 tablespoons salad dressing = 43 calories
                                            0 g protein
                                            6 g
                                            carbohydrate
                                            6 g fat
                                            49 mg
                                            sodium

One serving = 1 fat

One serving of salad with dressing = 299 calories
                                25 g protein
                                10 g carbohydrate
                                22 g fat
                                690 mg sodium

One serving = 3 medium-fat protein + 1 vegetable + 1 fat

Yogurt Cheese Sandwich Spread

½ cup yogurt cheese (see note)
2 tablespoons chopped raisins or
    dried apricots
1 tablespoon chopped pecans or
    sunflower seeds

Combine the ingredients in a small bowl and mix well. Spread on bread, rolls, or crackers.

Makes ⅔ cup

Note: To make ½ cup yogurt cheese, place 1 8-ounce carton plain or vanilla yogurt in a coffee filter inside a colander or strainer. Let stand at room temperature overnight to drain off the liquid. What remains in the filter is called *yogurt cheese.* (Always start with twice as much yogurt as the amount of cheese you'll need.)

One serving of ¼ cup = 155 calories
                        5 g protein
                        16 g carbohydrates
                        8 g fat
                        258 mg sodium

One serving = 1 low-fat protein + 1 fruit + 1 fat

Ricotta Cassata

1½ cups unbleached flour
½ teaspoon salt
¼ cup margarine or butter
3–4 tablespoons cold water
3 large egg whites
1½ pounds part-skim ricotta
cheese
¼ cup low-fat milk
¼ cup honey
1 teaspoon ground cinnamon

Preheat the oven to 375°F. Make the crust by combining the flour and salt in a bowl, then cutting in the margarine with a fork or pastry blender until it resembles coarse meal. Sprinkle 3 tablespoons water over the mixture, tossing with a fork until the pastry holds together; add the other tablespoon of water if needed. Place the dough on a lightly floured surface and roll into a large circle. Transfer to a 9-inch pie plate. Trim and crimp the edges. Combine the egg whites, cheese, milk, and honey in a blender or food processor. Process until smooth. Pour the mixture into the pastry shell. Sprinkle on the cinnamon. Bake for 10 minutes. Reduce the oven temperature to 350°F and bake for 25–30 minutes longer or until a knife inserted in the center comes out clean. Serve warm or cold.

Makes 8 servings.

One serving = 437 calories
23 g protein
18 g carbohydrate
8 g fat
597 mg sodium

One serving = 3 low-fat protein + 1 starch/bread + 1 fat

Cheese Soufflé

¼ cup margarine or butter
¼ cup all-purpose flour
1 teaspoon dry mustard
⅛ teaspoon freshly ground white
    pepper
1 cup skim milk
1 cup low-fat cottage cheese
3 large egg yolks
1 cup (¼ pound) freshly grated
    Parmesan cheese
6 large egg whites

Preheat the oven to 375°F. Combine the margarine, flour, mustard, and pepper in a skillet. Cook over medium heat 2 minutes. Gradually stir in the milk and cook until smooth and thick, about 3–5 minutes. Beat together the cottage cheese and egg yolks. Add to the milk mixture and stir in the cheese. In a bowl, beat the egg whites until stiff. Gently fold them into the cheese mixture. Pour into an ungreased straight-sided 1½-quart casserole or soufflé dish. Bake 30–40 minutes, until risen and set. Serve *immediately.*

Makes 6 servings

One serving = 382 calories
              25 g protein
              18 g carbohydrate
              20 g fat
              560 mg sodium

One serving = 3 medium-fat protein + 1 starch/bread + 1 fat

Banana French Toast

2 large eggs
½ cup skim milk
¼ teaspoon ground cinnamon
½ ripe banana
4 slices whole-grain bread

Beat the eggs, milk, cinnamon, and banana together in a food processor or blender. Dip the bread slices into the mixture and place on a nonstick griddle or skillet over medium-high heat and cook until browned on one side, about 3–5 minutes. Turn over and cook for about 2–3 minutes on the other side. Serve with diet syrup or unsweetened applesauce.

Makes 2 servings

One serving = 274 calories
12 g protein
37 g carbohydrate
6 g fat
410 mg sodium

One serving = 2 starch/bread + 1 medium-fat protein + ½ fruit

SALADS AND SALAD
DRESSINGS

Taco Salad

1 pound lean ground beef
½ cup chopped green bell pepper
1 cup (8 ounces) taco sauce
1 10-ounce bag tortilla chips
4 cups shredded lettuce
¼ pound Monterey Jack or
      cheddar cheese, grated (1 cup)
¼ cup chopped scallion
2 cups chopped fresh tomato
10 black olives, pitted and diced
1 ripe avocado, peeled, pitted,
      and chopped (optional)

Cook the ground beef and green pepper in a microwave-safe dish on HIGH for 5 minutes or until well cooked. Or cook in a skillet over medium-high heat, stirring often, for 5–10 minutes, until the meat is cooked through. Drain off the fat. Stir in about half the taco sauce.

Line a large serving plate with tortilla chips, reserving some for garnish around the sides. Top with lettuce and the meat mixture. Then layer on the cheese, scallion, and tomatoes. Pour on the rest of the taco sauce or pass it separately. Sprinkle black olives and avocado, if used, on top before serving.

Makes 6 servings

One serving = 505 calories
                26 g protein
                31 g carbohydrate
                22 g fat
                742 mg sodium

One serving = 3 medium-fat protein + 2 starch/bread + 2 vegetable + 2 fat

Pizza Salad

1 head iceberg lettuce
1 15-ounce can artichoke hearts,
    chilled
1½ cups cubed salami
½ cup pitted black olives
2 tablespoons pine nuts, toasted
2 ounces mozzarella cheese,
    cubed
2 tablespoons olive oil
½ cup canned tomato sauce
2 tablespoons wine vinegar
½ teaspoon Italian seasoning
⅛ teaspoon freshly ground black
    pepper

Cut the lettuce into bite-size chunks. Drain the artichoke hearts. Combine the lettuce, artichokes, salami, olives, pine nuts, and cheese in a bowl. Combine the oil, tomato sauce, vinegar, Italian herbs, and pepper in a jar. Shake well. Refrigerate for several hours to blend the flavors, then pour over the lettuce mixture. Toss.

Makes 6 servings

One serving = 297 calories
            22 g protein
            4 g carbohydrate
            28 g fat
            399 mg sodium

One serving = 3 high-fat protein + 1 vegetable + 1 fat

Hot German Chicken Salad

2 cups chopped celery
½ cup slivered almonds, toasted
1 2-ounce jar chopped
    pimientos, drained
1 green bell pepper, chopped
3 whole chicken breasts, cooked
    and the meat diced
½ cup mayonnaise
1 teaspoon German or other
    prepared mustard
¼ cup chopped scallion
½ teaspoon salt

Preheat the oven to 400°F. Mix the celery, almonds, pimiento, green pepper, and chicken together. Transfer to an oiled 2-quart casserole dish. Combine the mayonnaise, mustard, scallion, and salt in a mixing bowl and blend. Spread over the top of the chicken mixture. Bake, uncovered, for 20–25 minutes, until the topping is nicely browned.

Makes 6 servings

One serving = 271 calories
            24 g protein
            8 g carbohydrate
            19 g fat
            360 mg sodium

One serving = 3 low-fat protein + 1 vegetable + 2 fat

Turkey Waldorf Salad

1 pound cooked turkey breast
1 pear, cored and cubed
2 apples, cored and cubed
1 orange, peeled and cubed
1 cup seedless grapes
¼ cup chopped pecans
¼ cup orange juice
2 tablespoons olive oil
¼ cup mayonnaise or salad
    dressing
1 teaspoon prepared mustard
1 teaspoon dried tarragon leaves

Cut the turkey breast into bite-size cubes. Combine the turkey, fruits, and pecans in a bowl. Make the dressing by mixing the orange juice, olive oil, mayonnaise, mustard, and tarragon leaves in a bowl. Pour over the turkey and fruit and toss gently. Serve over lettuce.

Makes 6 servings

One serving = 231 calories
            19 g protein
            12 g carbohydrate
            21 g fat
            397 mg sodium

One serving = 3 low-fat protein + 1 fruit + 2 fat

Sautéed Salmon Spinach Salad

4 ¼-pound skinless salmon fillets
 or steaks
2 tablespoons olive oil
½ pound fresh spinach,
 thoroughly cleaned
¼ teaspoon salt
⅛ teaspoon freshly ground black
 pepper
½ cup chopped yellow onion
3 (about 1¼ pounds) fresh
 tomatoes, peeled, seeded (see
 Index), and cut into ½-inch
 pieces
1 tablespoon coarsely chopped
 flat-leaf parsley

Arrange the salmon on a plate. In a skillet, heat 1 table-spoon of the olive oil. When hot, sauté the spinach over medium heat for 1½ minutes. Mix in the salt and pepper and divide the spinach among four plates. Heat the remaining tablespoon of olive oil in the skillet. Sauté the onion and tomatoes over medium heat until the onion is tender, about 5 minutes. Push to one side and add the salmon. Sauté over medium heat until cooked through, about 5–6 minutes. Arrange the salmon on the spinach and top with the tomato and onions.

Makes 4 servings

One serving = 187 calories
    22 g protein
    4 g carbohydrate
    9 g fat
    181 mg sodium

One serving = 3 low-fat protein + 1 vegetable + 1 fat

Hot Scallops on Romaine Salad

1 pound bay scallops
½ teaspoon dried thyme leaves
½ teaspoon dried oregano leaves
1 teaspoon dried tarragon leaves
¼ teaspoon ground coriander
¼ teaspoon freshly ground white
pepper
1 tablespoon olive oil
Chopped romaine lettuce for
serving

Sprinkle the scallops with the thyme, oregano, tarragon, coriander, and white pepper. Heat the olive oil in a large skillet, add the scallops, and cook over high heat for 1–2 minutes, until the scallops are opaque. Divide the scallops among four plates lined with chopped romaine lettuce. Pour the cooking juices over the scallops and lettuce.

Makes 4 servings

One serving = 167 calories
22 g protein
3 g carbohydrate
4 g fat
84 mg sodium

One serving = 3 low-fat protein + 1 fat

Greek   Potato   Salad

2 tablespoons olive oil
2 tablespoons chopped scallion
3 tablespoons chopped green bell
    pepper
2 tablespoons wine vinegar
½ teaspoon dried oregano leaves
2 cups cubed cooked potatoes
2 tablespoons diced pitted black
    olives
¼ cup crumbled feta cheese
Cherry tomatoes and black
    olives for garnish

Combine the olive oil, scallion, green pepper, vinegar, and oregano in a skillet. Sauté over medium heat for about 3 minutes, until the green pepper is tender. Stir in the potatoes, olives, and feta cheese. Toss to mix. Serve warm with the cherry tomatoes and whole ripe olives.

Makes 4 servings

One serving = 177 calories
            8 g protein
            18 g carbohydrate
            12 g fat
            337 mg sodium

One serving = 1 starch/bread + 1 medium-fat protein + 1 fat

S w e e t   P o t a t o   S a l a d

2 quarts water
1 3-inch stick cinnamon
2 pounds sweet potatoes, peeled

ORANGE JUICE DRESSING
½ cup orange juice
¼ teaspoon ground cinnamon
½ cup low-fat vanilla yogurt
½ teaspoon salt

Bring the water and cinnamon to a boil in a pot large enough to hold the whole sweet potatoes. Add the potatoes, cover, and simmer for 30–45 minutes, until tender. Cool briefly and slice. Combine the dressing ingredients, then pour over the potatoes. Serve chilled or at room temperature.

Makes 8 servings

One serving = 91 calories
3 g protein
21 g carbohydrate
1 g fat
187 mg sodium

One serving = 1 starch/bread

Pasta Vegetable Salad

Grated zest of ½ medium-size
    orange
Juice of 1 medium-size orange
3 tablespoons vegetable oil
½ teaspoon dried dill weed
2 cups fusilli or rotini, cooked
    and drained
2 medium-size oranges, peeled
    and cut into bite-size pieces
2 cups broccoli florets, cooked
    and drained
½ cup sliced celery
¼ cup sliced scallion

In a large bowl, combine the orange zest and juice, oil, and dill. Add the remaining ingredients, toss gently, and chill.

Makes 4 servings

One serving = 212 calories
              5 g protein
              24 g carbohydrate
              11 g fat
              22 mg sodium

One serving = 1 starch/bread + 1 vegetable + 2 fat

Barley Pecan Salad

⅔ cup water
1 cup quick-cooking barley
1 cup chopped celery
½ cup finely chopped scallion
¼ cup chopped fresh parsley
¼ cup plain nonfat yogurt
¼ cup wine vinegar
1 tablespoon prepared mustard
¼ teaspoon freshly ground white
    pepper
2 11-ounce cans mandarin
    orange segments, drained (2
    cups)
⅓ cup coarsely chopped pecans

In a 2-quart saucepan, bring the water to a boil. Stir in the
barley, cover, and reduce the heat. Simmer for 10–12 minutes or until tender. Remove from the heat and let stand for
5 minutes. In a large bowl, combine the barley with the rest
of the ingredients. Mix well, cover, and chill for several hours
or overnight.

Makes 8 servings

One serving = 160 calories
                4 g protein
                29 g carbohydrate
                4 g fat
                91 mg sodium

One serving = 1 starch/bread + 1 fat

Seven-Layer Vegetable Salad

1½ cups halved cherry tomatoes
1 cup torn fresh spinach in bite-
    size pieces
1½ cups cauliflower florets
½ small head red cabbage,
    thinly sliced
1 cup sliced fresh mushrooms
2 small zucchini, sliced
½ cup mayonnaise
¼ cup buttermilk
1 clove garlic, minced
¼ cup crumbled blue cheese
Minced chives

Arrange the tomatoes, cut sides down, in the bottom of 2-quart soufflé dish or casserole. Layer the spinach, cauliflower, cabbage, mushrooms, and zucchini over the tomatoes. Mix together the mayonnaise, buttermilk, and garlic. Spread over the top of the salad. Sprinkle the dressing with the cheese and chives. Refrigerate, covered, for 8 hours or overnight. Toss before serving.

Makes 8 servings

One serving = 72 calories
            1 g protein
            9 g carbohydrate
            7 g fat
            59 mg sodium

One serving = 1 vegetable + 1 fat

Oriental Cabbage Salad

½ small head green cabbage
3 scallions, chopped
2 tablespoons dark sesame oil
2 tablespoons vinegar
1 teaspoon honey or sugar
    substitute
2 tablespoons sesame seeds,
    toasted
¼ cup slivered almonds, toasted

Combine the cabbage, scallions, oil, vinegar, and honey. Toss well and chill until ready to serve. Add the sesame seeds and almonds and toss again to mix before serving.

Makes 4 servings

One serving = 128 calories
              3 g protein
              8 g carbohydrate
              11 g fat
              159 mg sodium

One serving = 1 vegetable + 2 fat

English Pea Salad

1 10-ounce package frozen peas,
    cooked and chilled
1 2-ounce jar sliced pimientos,
    drained
½ cup finely chopped celery
¼ cup finely chopped onion
½ cup mayonnaise
3 tablespoons chopped fresh
    parsley
2 ounces cheddar cheese, cubed

Combine all the ingredients in a mixing bowl. Toss gently. Refrigerate to blend the flavors, at least 1 hour.

Makes 4 servings

One serving = 187 calories
                5 g protein
                23 g carbohydrate
                12 g fat
                398 mg sodium

One serving = 1 starch/bread + 1 vegetable + 1 fat + ½ high-fat protein

Broccoli Salad with Vinaigrette Dressing

3 cups broccoli florets and
peeled stems
⅓ cup vegetable oil
1 tablespoon wine vinegar
1 clove garlic, minced
¼ cup orange juice
1 teaspoon Dijon mustard
¼ cup grated carrot

Steam the broccoli just until fork-tender. In a large bowl, combine the oil, vinegar, garlic, orange juice, and mustard. Mix well. Add the broccoli to the dressing and toss to combine. Serve warm or at room temperature. Sprinkle the grated carrot over the top before serving.

Makes 4 servings

One serving = 58 calories
2 g protein
8 g carbohydrate
6 g fat
47 mg sodium

One serving = 1 vegetable + 1 fat

Mandarin Orange Spinach Salad

1 package sugar-free orange
    gelatin
½ cup low-fat vanilla yogurt
½ cup cold water
1 8-ounce can mandarin orange
    segments in light syrup,
    drained
½ pound fresh spinach leaves
2 tablespoons sliced almonds,
    toasted

Prepare the orange gelatin according to the package directions, *but* substitute the yogurt and cold water plus the drained orange segments for the cup of cold water called for. Chill the gelatin thoroughly.

Wash the spinach leaves and pat them dry. Line four salad plates or a serving platter with the spinach leaves. Unmold the gelatin or cut it into squares and arrange on the plates or platter. Top with the almonds just before serving.

Makes 4 servings

One serving = 171 calories
            2 g protein
            21 g carbohydrate
            7 g fat
            290 mg sodium

One serving = 2 fruit + 1 fat + 1 vegetable

Spinach Apple Salad

1 pound fresh spinach
1 cup chopped apple
½ cup chopped celery
¼ cup cider vinegar
¼ cup vegetable oil
1 teaspoon sugar
1 teaspoon caraway seeds
¼ teaspoon freshly ground white
*   pepper*

Remove the stems from the spinach; wash the leaves thoroughly and pat dry. Tear into bite-size pieces. Combine the spinach, apple, and celery in a large bowl. Combine the vinegar and remaining ingredients in a small saucepan and bring to a boil. Pour over the spinach mixture and toss well. Serve immediately.

Makes 4 servings

One serving = 61 calories
           1 g protein
           8 g carbohydrate
           4 g fat
           51 mg sodium

One serving = 2 vegetable + 1 fat + ½ fruit

Orange Ambrosia

2 heads Bibb lettuce
1 orange, peeled and cut into
    wedges
1 banana, peeled and sliced
1 apple, cored and sliced
1 tablespoon pine nuts, toasted
Raspberry vinegar
Olive oil

Arrange the lettuce leaves on four salad plates. Add the orange, banana, and apple. Top with pine nuts and pass the vinegar and oil.

Makes 4 servings

One serving = 94 calories
            1 g protein
            13 g carbohydrate
            4 g fat
            32 mg sodium

One serving = 1 vegetable + 1 fruit + 1 fat

Summer Delight Salad

1 grapefruit, sectioned
1 orange, sectioned
1 cucumber, sliced
1 red onion, sliced
1 apple, cored and cubed
½ cup orange juice
¼ cup wine vinegar
1 teaspoon sugar

Toss all the ingredients together. Cover and chill for 1-3 hours. Serve on lettuce.

Makes 4 servings

One serving = 48 calories
            0 g protein
            14 g carbohydrate
            0 g fat
            18 mg sodium

One serving = 1 fruit

Strawberry Salad

¼ cup sliced almonds
4 teaspoons sugar
2 cups mixed salad greens
1 rib celery, chopped
2 scallions, chopped
2 cups sliced fresh strawberries
1 8-ounce can mandarin orange
    segments in light syrup,
    drained
¼ cup vegetable oil
1 tablespoon cider vinegar

Cook the almonds and 2 teaspoons of the sugar in a microwave-safe dish on HIGH for 1 minute. Cool. Place the salad greens, celery, scallions, strawberries, and mandarin orange segments in a salad bowl. Combine the vegetable oil, remaining 2 teaspoons sugar, and cider vinegar and toss the salad with this dressing. Top with the sugared almonds.

Makes 4 servings

One serving = 172 calories
              1 g protein
              18 g carbohydrate
              12 g fat
              52 mg sodium

One serving = 1 fruit + 1 vegetable + 2 fat

Tofu Ginger Dressing

½ pound tofu, drained
3 tablespoons fresh lemon juice
1 tablespoon dark sesame oil
1 ¼-inch piece fresh ginger,
    peeled and chopped, or ½
    teaspoon ground ginger
1 small clove garlic (optional)
½ cup plain low-fat yogurt

Process the tofu, lemon juice, sesame oil, ginger, and garlic in a food processor or blender until smooth. Pour into a bowl, stir in the yogurt, and mix well. Serve over vegetable salads or chicken salad.

Makes 2 cups

One serving of 2 tablespoons = 52 calories
                            6 g protein
                            7 g carbohydrate
                            2 g fat
                            278 mg sodium

One serving = 1 low-fat protein

Low-Fat
Thousand Island Dressing

> 1 cup peeled, seeded (see Index),
>   and diced fresh tomato
> 1 large clove garlic
> ½ teaspoon salt
> ¼ teaspoon freshly ground black
>   pepper
> ¼ teaspoon dry mustard
> 2 tablespoons fresh lemon juice
> 4–5 sprigs fresh parsley
> 1 cup low-fat cottage cheese
> ¼ cup dill pickle juice
> 2 tablespoons finely chopped dill
>   pickles
> 1 large egg, hard-cooked and
>   chopped fine

Blend the tomatoes, garlic, salt, pepper, dry mustard, and lemon juice in a blender or food processor until smooth. Pour into a bowl. Blend the cottage cheese and pickle juice until smooth. Beat together the tomato puree, cottage cheese puree, pickles, and egg. Chill to blend flavors for at least 1 hour before serving.

Makes 2½ cups

One serving of ¼ cup = 42 calories
                         4 g protein
                         10 g carbohydrate
                         4 g fat
                         210 mg sodium

One serving = ½ medium-fat protein

Almost Zero Salad Dressing

½ cup tomato juice
2 tablespoons vinegar or fresh
  lemon juice
1 clove garlic, minced
¼ teaspoon freshly ground
  pepper
1 teaspoon finely chopped fresh
  parsley
1 tablespoon minced yellow
  onion

Combine all the ingredients in a jar and shake well. Refrigerate until needed. Serve over salad greens.

Makes ½ cup

One serving of 2 tablespoons = 6 calories

    0 g protein
    25 g carbohydrate
    0 g fat
    31 mg sodium

One serving = free

VEGETABLES

Lima Beans and Tomatoes

1 15-ounce can lima beans
2 tablespoons chopped scallion
1 tablespoon chopped fresh
    parsley
¼ cup chopped green bell pepper
1 cup chopped fresh tomato
¼ teaspoon chili powder

Combine the ingredients in a 2-quart baking dish. Bake for 40–45 minutes.

Makes 4 servings

One serving = 105 calories
            7 g protein
            22 g carbohydrate
            0 fat
            111 mg sodium

One serving = 1 starch/bread + 1 vegetable

Brussels Sprouts with Almonds

1 pound fresh brussels sprouts
¼ cup slivered almonds
1 tablespoon olive oil
¼ teaspoon salt (optional)

Trim the brussels sprouts and steam until tender. Brown the almonds in the olive oil in a skillet over medium heat for about 3 minutes. Add the sprouts and salt, if desired. Heat until ready to serve.

Makes 3 servings

One serving = 105 calories
2 g protein
6 g carbohydrate
9 g fat
105 mg sodium

One serving = 1 vegetable + 2 fat

Red Cabbage with Raisins

1 large head red cabbage
2 tablespoons vegetable oil
2 apples, cored and chopped
½ teaspoon salt
1 teaspoon ground nutmeg
¼ cup cider vinegar
2 tablespoons honey
¼ cup raisins

Core and shred the cabbage. Heat the vegetable oil in a skillet over medium heat and add the cabbage. Toss the cabbage to coat with vegetable oil. Add the remaining ingredients, cover, and simmer over medium heat for about 1 hour, until the cabbage is tender. You may have to add water or apple juice to prevent sticking during cooking.

Makes 6 servings

One serving = 78 calories
1 g protein
10 g carbohydrate
6 g fat
72 mg sodium

One serving = 1 vegetable + 1 fat

Frosted Cauliflower

1 head cauliflower
¼ cup water
½ cup plain low-fat yogurt
½ teaspoon dry mustard
¼ teaspoon onion salt or onion
     powder
¼ teaspoon celery seeds
1 cup grated cheddar cheese

Wash and core the cauliflower. Place it stem end down in a microwave-safe 2-quart casserole dish. Add the water and cover. Microwave on HIGH until tender, about 10 minutes. Combine the yogurt, mustard, onion salt, and celery seeds in a bowl. Spread over the cauliflower. Sprinkle on the cheese. Microwave on HIGH, uncovered, for 2 minutes or until the cheese is melted.

To prepare on the stove, steam the cauliflower until fork-tender, spread on the yogurt cheese topping, and place under a preheated broiler just until the cheese melts.

Makes 6 servings

One serving = 62 calories
           4 g protein
           6 g carbohydrate
           4 g fat
           418 mg sodium

One serving = 1 vegetable + ½ high-fat protein

Orange Dill Carrots

2 cups sliced carrots
1 teaspoon margarine
½ cup (3 medium-size) fresh
    orange segments
½ teaspoon dried dill weed

Steam the carrots until tender. Combine the cooked carrots, margarine, orange sections, and dill in a saucepan. Cook over low heat until all the ingredients are heated through.

Makes 4 servings

One serving = 76 calories
                1 g protein
                12 g carbohydrate
                2 g fat
                21 mg sodium

One serving = 1 vegetable + ½ fruit

Scalloped Potatoes

2 medium-size potatoes, peeled
    and sliced thin
2 tablespoons all-purpose flour
1/4 teaspoon salt
Dash freshly ground white
    pepper
1/2 cup low-fat milk

Preheat the oven to 400°F. Coat the potato slices with flour, salt, and pepper. Place in a lightly oiled 2-quart baking dish. Pour the milk over the top, cover, and bake for 30–40 minutes, until the potatoes are tender.

Makes 2 servings

One serving = 91 calories
            3 g protein
            18 g carbohydrate
            2 g fat
            86 mg sodium

One serving = 1 starch/bread

Savory   Herbed   Potatoes

4 (about 1½ pounds) medium-
    size potatoes
1 16-ounce can whole tomatoes,
    drained
½ cup chopped yellow onion
2 cloves garlic, minced
¼ cup dried bread crumbs
¼ teaspoon dried thyme leaves

Peel and slice the potatoes. Place in a 2-quart microwave-safe dish. Add the tomatoes, onion, and garlic. Sprinkle on the bread crumbs and thyme. Cover and microwave on HIGH for 10 minutes or until the potatoes are tender.

To prepare in a conventional oven, preheat the oven to 350°F. Combine the ingredients in a lightly oiled 2-quart casserole dish, cover, and bake for 30 minutes or until the potatoes are tender.

Makes 4 servings

One serving = 95 calories
              2 g protein
              17 g carbohydrate
              0 g fat
              218 mg sodium

One serving = 1 starch/bread + 1 vegetable

Broiled Tomato with Pesto

> *3 fresh tomatoes*
> *2 cloves garlic*
> *1 cup fresh basil leaves*
> *2 tablespoons olive oil*
> *¼ cup freshly grated Parmesan*
>   *cheese*
> *2 tablespoons pine nuts*

Cut the tomatoes in half. Combine the rest of the ingredients in a blender or food processor and puree until smooth. Spoon the mixture onto the top of each tomato half. Broil the tomatoes about 3 inches from the heat until lightly browned, about 3–5 minutes.

Makes 6 servings

One serving = 82 calories
                3 g protein
                8 g carbohydrate
                8 g fat
                99 mg sodium

One serving = 1 vegetable + 1 fat

Zucchini Medley

3 cups zucchini chunks
1 small yellow onion, sliced
1 medium-size fresh tomato,
*   chopped*
½ cup fresh mushroom caps
½ teaspoon dried basil leaves
2 ounces low-fat cheddar cheese,
*   grated (½ cup)*

Place all the ingredients except the cheese in a microwave-safe 2-quart casserole dish. Microwave on HIGH for 7–10 minutes, until the vegetables are fork-tender. Add the cheese and microwave on HIGH for 30 seconds. Let stand for 2–3 minutes before serving.

To cook on the stove, steam the vegetables until fork-tender, then toss with the basil and cheese. Keep warm until serving time.

Makes 4 servings

One serving = 39 calories
          3 g protein
          7 g carbohydrate
          3 g fat
          191 mg sodium

One serving = 1 vegetable

Baked Vegetable Medley

4 medium-size potatoes
4 parsnips
4 medium-size yellow onions
1 pound acorn or butternut
     squash
Salt and freshly ground black
     pepper to taste

Preheat the oven to 400°F. Wash and peel all the vegetables. Cut into serving pieces. Lightly oil a 2-quart casserole dish and add the vegetables to it. Sprinkle on salt and pepper. Cover and bake for about 1 hour or until the vegetables are tender.

Makes 4 servings

One serving = 155 calories
             4 g protein
             27 g carbohydrate
             1 g fat
             47 mg sodium

One serving = 2 starch/bread

BREADS

Hearty   Oatmeal   Bread

*5¼–5¾ cups sifted all-purpose
    flour
1 teaspoon salt
2¼ cups milk
¼ cup margarine or butter
¼ cup sugar
2 ¼-ounce envelopes active dry
    yeast
2 cups quick-cooking or old-
    fashioned oats
1 tablespoon caraway seeds*

Stir together 2 cups of the flour and the salt in a large bowl.
Heat the milk, margarine, and sugar together over low heat
until the margarine is soft. Add the liquid to the flour. Beat
for 2 minutes on the medium speed of an electric mixer or
300 strokes by hand.

Combine 1 cup of flour and the yeast. Add to the batter.
Beat for 2 minutes on medium speed, or 300 strokes by
hand. Stir in the oats and caraway with a wooden spoon. Stir
in enough additional flour to make a stiff dough. Turn out
onto a floured board. Knead until smooth, 8–10 minutes.
Place in a greased large bowl. Brush the top with vegetable
oil. Cover with a damp kitchen towel and let rise in a warm
place until double in size, about 1 hour.

Punch the dough down. Divide it in half and shape to
form two loaves. Place in two greased 8½" × 4½" loaf pans.
Brush with melted margarine or butter. Cover and let rise
until nearly double in size, about 1 hour. When almost
doubled, preheat the oven to 375°F. Bake for about 40 minutes or until brown. Cool before slicing.

Makes 2 loaves

One slice = 78 calories
             2 g protein
             16 g carbohydrate
             1 g fat
             181 mg sodium

One slice = 1 starch/bread

Sunflower Loaf

1 ¼-ounce envelope active dry
   yeast
1 teaspoon sugar
1¼ cups warm (105–115°F)
   water
¼ cup honey
½ cup buttermilk
1 teaspoon salt
4 cups whole-wheat flour
½ cup sunflower seeds, toasted
1 large egg yolk
1 tablespoon milk
½ cup sunflower seeds,
   untoasted

Dissolve the yeast and sugar in the warm water in a large bowl. Let the mixture stand for about 10 minutes, until the yeast starts to foam. Add the honey, buttermilk, and salt. Blend well. Add the flour and toasted sunflower seeds and mix well. (The dough will be sticky.) Turn the dough out onto a lightly floured board and knead it for about 10 minutes. Shape it into a ball. Coat the dough lightly with flour and place it on a baking sheet. Cover it with a damp cloth and let rise in a warm place for 20 minutes. Knead the dough again and form into a ball. Let the dough rise, covered, a second time for 40 minutes.

Shape the dough into a loaf. Mix the egg yolk with the milk and brush the top of the loaf with the mixture. Sprinkle the untoasted sunflower seeds on a work surface and roll the top of the loaf in them. Place the loaf in an oiled 9″ × 4″ loaf pan. Cover the pan with a damp cloth and let rise for 15 minutes or until the dough is about 1 inch over the top of the pan. When almost finished rising, preheat the oven to 375°F. Bake for about 40 minutes or until the bread sounds hollow when the bottom is tapped.

Makes 1 large loaf

One slice about ½ inch thick = 85 calories

         4 g protein

         18 g carbohydrate

         1 g fat

         129 mg sodium

One slice = 1 starch/bread

Roman Sandwich Bread

1 ¼-ounce envelope active dry
    yeast
1¼ cups warm (105–115°F)
    water
2 tablespoons margarine or
    butter
2 teaspoons salt
2 tablespoons sugar
3 cups all-purpose flour
1 large egg white
2 tablespoons water
1 tablespoon dried oregano
    leaves
¼ teaspoon salt
⅛ teaspoon freshly ground black
    pepper

Dissolve the yeast in the warm water in a large bowl. Add the margarine, 2 teaspoons salt, sugar, and 1½ cups flour. Beat for 2 minutes at medium speed on an electric mixer or 300 strokes by hand. Add the remaining flour and beat in with a spoon. Cover with a damp cloth and let rise in a warm place until double in size, about 30 minutes. Stir the batter down by beating 25 strokes. Spread the batter evenly in a lightly oiled 9-inch square pan. Combine the egg white and 2 table-spoons water. Brush on top of the batter. Sprinkle with oregano, salt, and pepper. Let rise until double, about 40 minutes. When almost double, preheat the oven to 350°F. Bake for 45–50 minutes or until brown. Remove from the pan and cool on a rack. Slice in half horizontally, then cut into 8 wedges. Fill with sandwich ingredients as desired.

Makes 8 servings

One serving = 147 calories
            2 g protein
            32 g carbohydrate
            2 g fat
            310 mg sodium

One serving = 2 starch/bread

Banana Nut Bread

⅓ cup vegetable oil
⅓ cup sugar
1 teaspoon vanilla extract
1 large egg
1 very ripe banana
1½ cups whole-wheat flour
2 teaspoons baking powder
½ teaspoon baking soda
½ teaspoon ground cinnamon
½ cup low-fat milk
½ cup chopped nuts

Preheat the oven to 350°F. Cream together the oil, sugar, vanilla, egg, and banana. Add the flour, baking powder, baking soda, and cinnamon. Blend lightly while stirring in the milk and nuts. Pour the batter into a lightly oiled 9″ × 4″ loaf pan. Bake for 45–50 minutes, until browned and batter pulls away from sides of pan.

Makes 12 servings

One serving = 174 calories
            2 g protein
            28 g carbohydrate
            6 g fat
            184 mg sodium

One serving = 1 starch/bread + 1 fat + 1 fruit

Prune Bread

2½ cups all-purpose flour
1 teaspoon baking soda
2 teaspoons baking powder
28 (1¾ cups) pitted prunes
½ cup boiling water
½ cup sugar
2 large eggs
¼ cup vegetable oil
1 cup orange juice

Preheat the oven to 350°F. Oil and flour two 9″ × 4″ loaf pans. Place the flour, baking soda, baking powder, and salt in a bowl. Stir to blend. Process the prunes and boiling water in a food processor or blender for 10 seconds. Add the sugar and eggs and process for 1 minute. Add the oil and process for 1 minute longer. Add the orange juice.

Add the prune mixture to the flour mixture. Beat well. Divide the batter between the prepared pans. Bake for 1 hour, until browned. Cool the loaves for 10 minutes before removing from the pans.

Makes 2 loaves

One slice about ½ inch thick = 92 calories
                              2 g protein
                              21 g carbohydrate
                              3 g fat
                              84 mg sodium

One slice = 1 starch/bread

New England Election Cake

1 ¼-ounce envelope active dry
    yeast
¼ cup warm (105–115°F) water
½ cup plus 1 tablespoon sugar
¾ cup milk, heated to lukewarm
3½ cups all-purpose flour, sifted
½ cup margarine or butter,
    softened
2 large eggs
2 teaspoons fresh lemon juice
1 teaspoon grated lemon peel
1 cup dried currants or raisins
½ teaspoon salt
¾ teaspoon ground nutmeg or
    mace
1 teaspoon ground cinnamon
½ cup powdered sugar
2–3 tablespoons fresh lemon or
    orange juice

Dissolve the yeast in the warm water in a large bowl. Stir in 1 tablespoon of the sugar and set aside for about 10 minutes, until the mixture bubbles.

Stir the lukewarm milk into the yeast mixture. Add 1 cup of the flour and beat until blended. Cover and let rise in a warm place until doubled in size, about 1 hour.

Cream together the butter and remaining ½ cup of sugar until light and fluffy. Add the eggs and beat well. Stir in the 2 teaspoons lemon juice and grated peel. Add the yeast mixture and beat to mix. Stir in the currants.

Combine the remaining 2½ cups flour with the salt, nutmeg, and cinnamon. Gradually stir the flour mixture into the batter, beating well.

Pour the batter into a well-oiled 10-inch tube pan. Cover with a damp cloth and let rise in a warm place for 3 hours or until doubled in bulk.

Place the pan in a cold oven. Set the oven at 300°F and bake for 35 minutes. Raise the oven temperature to 350°F and bake for 30 minutes more.

Let the cake cool for 10 minutes in the pan, then transfer to a rack. Meanwhile, combine the powdered sugar with the lemon or orange juice to make a glaze. Pour the glaze over the top of the warm cake, letting it drizzle down the sides.

Makes 12 servings

One serving = 171 calories
                        2 g protein
                        28 g carbohydrate
                        7 g fat
                        178 mg sodium

One serving = 1 starch/bread + 1 fat + 1 fruit

Polish Poppy Seed Bread

3 cups all-purpose flour
½ teaspoon salt
1½ teaspoons baking powder
½ cup sugar
2 teaspoons vanilla extract
1½ cups skim milk
¾ cup vegetable oil
½ cup frozen orange juice
    concentrate, defrosted
2 tablespoons poppy seeds
3 large eggs
1½ teaspoons almond extract
1 tablespoon finely grated orange
    zest
2 tablespoons confectioners'
    sugar

Preheat the oven to 350°F. Combine all the ingredients except the orange zest and confectioners' sugar in a large mixing bowl. Beat for 2 minutes on medium speed of an electric mixer or 300 strokes by hand.

Lightly oil two 9″ × 4″ loaf pans. Divide the batter between the pans and bake for 55 minutes. Remove from the pans and sprinkle with orange zest and confectioners' sugar while warm.

Makes 2 loaves

One slice about ½ inch thick = 124 calories
                          2 g protein
                          16 g carbohydrate
                          5 g fat
                          45 mg sodium

One slice = 1 starch/bread

C o r n   M u f f i n s

2 cups cornmeal
¼ teaspoon salt
3 teaspoons baking powder
2 tablespoons sugar
1 large egg
2 tablespoons vegetable oil
¾ cup water

Preheat the oven to 400°F. Combine all the ingredients in a mixing bowl. Stir to blend. Pour into nine lightly oiled muffin cups. Bake for 15–20 minutes or until golden brown.

Makes 9 muffins

One muffin = 121 calories
              2 g protein
              18 g carbohydrate
              6 g fat
              203 mg sodium

One muffin = 1 starch/bread + 1 fat

Dilly Corn Muffins

1 cup all-purpose flour
1 tablespoon sugar
1 tablespoon baking powder
1 large egg
½ cup low-fat milk
2 tablespoons vegetable oil
½ cup cornmeal
2 tablespoons minced scallion
2 tablespoons minced fresh
    parsley or 2 teaspoons dried
2 tablespoons fresh dill weed or
    2 teaspoons dried

Preheat the oven to 400°F. Combine the flour, sugar, and baking powder in a bowl. Stir to mix. Beat the egg, milk, and oil together. Add to the flour mixture along with the rest of the ingredients. Mix just until the batter is blended. Fill eight lightly oiled or paper-lined muffin cups about three-quarters full. Bake for 12–15 minutes or until brown.

Makes 8 muffins

One muffin = 97 calories
            2 g protein
            18 g carbohydrate
            4 g fat
            94 mg sodium

One muffin = 1 starch/bread + 1 fat

B r a n   M u f f i n s

¾ cup whole-wheat flour
⅓ cup wheat or rice bran
1 tablespoon baking powder
2 tablespoons sugar or honey
2 tablespoons vegetable oil
⅔ cup soy milk or skim milk
¼ cup raisins

Preheat the oven to 400°F. Combine all the ingredients in a mixing bowl and stir to combine. Spoon into six lightly oiled muffin cups. Bake for 15–20 minutes or until brown.

Makes 6 muffins

One muffin = 132 calories
2 g protein
22 g carbohydrate
6 g fat
183 mg sodium

One muffin = 1 starch/bread + 1 fat + 1 fruit

Crunchy Oat Bran Muffins

1 cup rolled oats
1 cup oat bran
⅓ cup sugar
1 tablespoon baking powder
½ teaspoon ground cinnamon
¼ teaspoon salt
¾ cup skim milk
2 large egg whites or 1 large egg
2 tablespoons vegetable oil
⅓ cup chopped peanuts
½ cup chopped apple

Preheat the oven to 400°F. Combine all the ingredients in a large bowl. Stir just enough to moisten. Fill 12 lightly oiled or paper-lined muffin cups. Bake for 15–20 minutes or until brown.

Makes 12 muffins

One muffin = 115 calories
                  4 g protein
                  19 g carbohydrate
                  6 g fat
                  184 mg sodium

One muffin = 1 starch/bread + 1 fat

Zucchini Carrot Muffins

1¾ cups rolled oats
1 cup all-purpose flour
½ cup sugar
1 tablespoon baking powder
¼ teaspoon ground nutmeg
1 cup (about 2 large) grated
    carrots
½ cup (about 1 medium-size)
    grated zucchini
⅔ cup skim milk
3 tablespoons vegetable oil
2 large egg whites or 1 large egg
¼ cup wheat germ
1 tablespoon chopped nuts

Preheat the oven to 400°F. Combine the oats, flour, sugar, baking powder, and nutmeg in a large bowl. Mix well. Add the carrots, zucchini, milk, oil, and egg whites. Mix just until moistened. Fill 12 lightly oiled or paper-lined muffin cups almost full. Combine the wheat germ and nuts and sprinkle evenly over the batter. Bake for 20–25 minutes or until golden brown.

Makes 12 muffins

One muffin = 164 calories
              5 g protein
              23 g carbohydrate
              6 g fat
              187 mg sodium

One muffin = 1 starch/bread + 1 fat + 1 vegetable

Carrot Muffins

1 cup all-purpose flour
⅓ cup sugar
2 teaspoons baking powder
1 teaspoon ground cinnamon
¼ teaspoon salt
½ cup bran or 1 cup bran cereal
½ cup raisins
1½ cups (2 large) grated carrots
¼ cup vegetable oil
1 large egg
½ cup milk

Preheat the oven to 400°F. Stir together the flour, sugar, baking powder, cinnamon, salt, bran, and raisins. Add the carrots, oil, egg, and milk. Mix just until the ingredients are blended. Pour the batter into nine lightly oiled or paper-lined muffin cups. Bake for 15–20 minutes, until brown. Cool for 5 minutes before removing from the tins.

Makes 9 muffins

One muffin = 98 calories
            2 g protein
            19 g carbohydrate
            7 g fat
            174 mg sodium

One muffin = 1 starch/bread + 1 fat

Cocoa Muffins

1 cup all-purpose flour
⅓ cup sugar
¼ cup unsweetened cocoa
    powder
2 teaspoons baking powder
½ cup milk
⅓ cup vegetable oil
1 large egg
½ cup raisins
½ cup chopped walnuts

Preheat the oven to 350°F. Combine the flour, sugar, cocoa, and baking powder in a bowl. Add the milk, oil, and egg. Stir just until moistened. Fold in the raisins and nuts. Spoon the batter into 12 lightly oiled or paper-lined muffin cups. Bake for 15–20 minutes, until brown.

Makes 12 muffins

One muffin = 159 calories
             2 g protein
             20 g carbohydrate
             12 g fat
             167 mg sodium

One muffin = 1 starch/bread + 2 fat

Banana Chocolate Muffins

⅓ *cup vegetable oil*
⅓ *cup sugar*
1 *large egg*
¼ *cup skim milk*
1 *ripe banana, mashed*
1 *cup plus 2 tablespoons all-*
    purpose flour
1 *teaspoon baking powder*
½ *teaspoon baking soda*
½ *cup chopped nuts*
½ *cup semisweet chocolate chips*

Preheat the oven to 350°F. Combine the oil, sugar, and egg in a bowl. Beat until creamy. Stir in the milk and mashed banana. Add the flour, baking powder, and baking soda. Fold in the nuts and chocolate. Fill eight lightly oiled or paper-lined muffin cups two-thirds full. Bake for 12–15 minutes, until brown.

Makes 8 muffins

One muffin = 109 calories
          2 g protein
          18 g carbohydrate
          7 g fat
          310 mg sodium

One serving = 1 starch/bread + 1 fat

S c o n e s

3 cups all-purpose flour
4½ teaspoons baking powder
¼ teaspoon salt
¼ cup margarine or butter
1 cup milk

Preheat the oven to 450°F. Combine the flour, baking powder, and salt in a bowl. Stir to mix. Cut in the margarine with a pastry blender or fork until the mixture resembles coarse meal. Add the milk and stir until the dough holds together. Knead on a clean surface for about 3 minutes. Roll out the dough to ½ inch thickness. Cut into rounds with a biscuit cutter and place on a lightly oiled baking sheet. Bake for 10–15 minutes or until golden brown.

Makes 12 scones

One scone = 109 calories
             2 g protein
             18 g carbohydrate
             8 g fat
             269 mg sodium

One scone = 1 starch/bread + 1 fat

Chelsea Buns

Prepared dough for Scones
  (preceding recipe)
1 tablespoon margarine or butter
1 tablespoon sugar
1½ teaspoons ground cinnamon

Preheat the oven to 425°F. Melt the butter, sugar, and cinnamon in a saucepan on the stove or in a custard cup in the microwave. Roll out the scone dough into a thin 9″ × 12″ rectangle. Spread the cinnamon mixture over the dough. Roll up and cut into 12 slices about ½ inch thick. Place on a lightly oiled baking sheet. Bake for 10–12 minutes, until brown.

Makes 12 buns

One bun = 134 calories
          2 g protein
          22 g carbohydrate
          9 g fat
          272 mg sodium

One bun = 1 starch/bread + 1 fat

D a t e   N u t   R o l l s

1 8-ounce package refrigerated
    crescent rolls
¼ cup honey crunch wheat germ
1 teaspoon ground cinnamon
½ cup chopped pitted dates or
    raisins
¼ cup chopped walnuts

Separate the crescent rolls into triangles on a flat surface. Sprinkle on the wheat germ, cinnamon, chopped dates, and walnuts. Roll up the rolls and place seam side down on a microwave-safe plate. Microwave on HIGH for 3–4 minutes, until thoroughly cooked. Or bake on a baking sheet at 375°F for 10–12 minutes, until browned.

Makes 8 rolls

One roll = 221 calories
        2 g protein
        29 g carbohydrate
        11 g fat
        315 mg sodium

One roll = 1 starch/bread + 1 fruit + 2 fat

Prune Orange Breakfast Rolls

> 1 ¼-ounce envelope active dry
>   yeast
> 3 tablespoons warm (105–115°F)
>   water
> 3 tablespoons orange juice
> 1 tablespoon sugar
> 2 teaspoons grated orange peel
> 1 large egg
> 1¾ cups sifted all-purpose flour
> 3 tablespoons melted margarine
>   or butter

PRUNE-ORANGE FILLING
> ¾ cup pitted prunes
> ⅓ cup orange juice
> 1 tablespoon sugar
> 1 teaspoon grated orange peel

Sprinkle the yeast over the warm water in a large bowl; let stand for 5 minutes to soften. Add the orange juice, sugar, orange peel, and egg. Stir in 1 cup of the flour and mix until smooth. Add the margarine. Gradually beat in the remaining flour to make a soft dough. Cover with a kitchen towel and let rise in a warm place until double in size, about 1 hour.

Meanwhile, prepare the filling. Cut the prunes into small pieces and mix with the juice in a small saucepan; simmer for 4–5 minutes or until the prunes are soft and the liquid has been absorbed. Remove from the heat and stir in the sugar and orange peel. Let cool while the dough rises.

When the dough has almost doubled, preheat the oven to 375°F. When fully risen, punch it down; turn out onto a floured board. Roll into an 8" × 12" rectangle. Spread the filling on the dough, leaving about a ½-inch edge uncovered on the long sides. Starting from a long side, roll up the dough, pinching the ends together to seal. Cut into 12 1-inch slices and put cut side down in a greased 8-inch layer pan. Let rise until double in size, about 45 minutes. Bake for 35–40 minutes or until nicely browned.

Makes 12 rolls

One roll = 169 calories
            2 g protein
            28 g carbohydrate
            8 g fat
            141 mg sodium

One roll = 1 starch/bread + 1 fat + 1 fruit

A b e l s k i v e r   P a n c a k e s

3 large eggs, separated
½ teaspoon salt
2 cups buttermilk
2 cups all-purpose flour
1 teaspoon baking soda
1 teaspoon baking powder
2 teaspoons sugar
Margarine or butter
½ cup chopped apple or
    blueberries

In a mixing bowl, combine the egg yolks, salt, and butter-milk. Beat well. Add the flour, baking soda, baking powder, and sugar and beat in. In a separate bowl, beat the egg whites until stiff. Gently fold into the batter. Heat an abel-skiver pan (see note) over high heat. Place a small amount of margarine or butter in each cup. Fill two-thirds full of batter and sprinkle on the chopped apple or blueberries. Fry until browned on the edges, about 2 minutes. Flip over and cook for about 1 minute more. Transfer to a warm platter. Serve with cinnamon-flavored sugar substitute sprinkled on top.

Makes 12 servings

Note: An abelskiver pan is similar to a pancake griddle with muffin-cup-like indentations. If unavailable, use a pancake griddle and cook like pancakes.

One serving of 3 pancakes = 106 calories
                            2 g protein
                            17 g carbohydrate
                            4 g fat
                            206 mg sodium

One serving = 1 starch/bread + 1 fat

Pecan Waffles

2 large eggs
2 cups buttermilk
1 tablespoon sugar
1 teaspoon baking soda
2 cups all-purpose flour
2 teaspoons baking powder
¼ cup melted margarine or
   butter
¼ cup chopped pecans

Heat a waffle iron while you mix the batter. Beat the eggs, buttermilk, and sugar together. Add the baking soda, flour, baking powder, and margarine. Beat until smooth. Pour the batter onto a heated greased waffle iron. Sprinkle ½ table-spoon pecans onto each waffle. Bake in waffle iron until golden brown, about 3–5 minutes.

Makes 8 waffles

One waffle = 164 calories
              4 g protein
              21 g carbohydrate
              11 g fat
              274 mg sodium

One serving = 1 starch/bread + 2 fat

DESSERTS AND
SNACKS

Chocolate Carrot Cake

2½ cups all-purpose flour
1 cup sugar
½ cup unsweetened cocoa
    powder
2 teaspoons baking soda
1 teaspoon ground cinnamon
½ teaspoon ground nutmeg
2 8-ounce cans juice-packed
    crushed pineapple
¾ cup vegetable oil
3 large eggs
2 cups (about 6) shredded
    carrots

Preheat the oven to 350°F. Combine the flour, sugar, cocoa, baking soda, cinnamon, and nutmeg in a large mixing bowl. Stir in the undrained pineapple, oil, eggs, and carrots. Beat until blended. Pour the batter into an oiled 10-inch tube pan. Bake for 40–45 minutes or until a toothpick inserted in the center comes out clean. Cool for 10 minutes in the pan, then remove the cake from the pan and cool completely on a rack.

Makes 20 servings

One serving = 125 calories
                3 g protein
                18 g carbohydrate
                6 g fat
                134 mg sodium

One serving = 1 starch/bread + 1 fat

Carrot Bundt Cake

¾ cup vegetable oil
¾ cup sugar
2 large eggs
1 cup (about 3) grated carrots
2½ cups unbleached all-purpose
    flour
1 tablespoon baking powder
1 teaspoon ground cinnamon
¼ teaspoon ground allspice
⅛ teaspoon ground cloves
1 cup orange juice
½ cup finely chopped walnuts

Preheat the oven to 325°F. Cream the oil, sugar, and eggs together in a large bowl. Stir in the carrots. Add the flour, baking powder, cinnamon, allspice, and cloves. Stir in the orange juice. Fold in the nuts. Pour the batter into a greased and floured 10-inch tube or Bundt cake pan. Bake for 45–55 minutes, until browned and toothpick inserted into center comes out clean. Cool for 5 minutes on a rack before removing from the pan.

Makes 16 servings

One serving = 222 calories
            2 g protein
            28 g carbohydrate
            12 g fat
            319 mg sodium

One serving = 1 starch/bread + 1 fruit + 2 fat

Pumpkin Pudding Cake

2 cups all-purpose flour
⅓ cup sugar
1 teaspoon baking powder
½ teaspoon baking soda
½ teaspoon ground cinnamon
¼ teaspoon ground cloves
½ cup canned pumpkin
⅓ cup vegetable oil
1 large egg
½ cup raisins
1 cup orange juice or water
½ cup chopped walnuts

Preheat the oven to 350°F. Combine the flour, sugar, baking powder, baking soda, cinnamon, and cloves in a bowl. Stir to mix. Add the pumpkin, oil, egg, raisins, and orange juice. Beat for 3 minutes. Lightly oil a tube pan. Sprinkle in the nuts. Pour the cake batter over the nuts. Bake for 40–50 minutes, until browned. Cool in the pan for 5 minutes before removing. Serve warm with a spoonful of yogurt.

Makes 12 servings

One serving = 195 calories
            3 g protein
            28 g carbohydrate
            7 g fat
            62 mg sodium

One serving = 1 starch/bread + 1 fruit + 1 fat

Sponge Cake with Strawberries

3 large eggs, separated
¾ cup confectioners' sugar
1 teaspoon vanilla extract
½ teaspoon grated orange peel
2 tablespoons hot water
1 cup all-purpose flour
1 teaspoon baking powder
1 cup sliced strawberries
½ cup vanilla yogurt

Preheat the oven to 325°F. Beat the egg yolks and confectioners' sugar together until smooth. Add the vanilla, orange zest, and hot water. Beat in the flour and baking powder a little at a time.

In a separate bowl, beat the egg whites until stiff peaks form. Fold the whites into the egg yolk mixture. Pour the batter gently into two 8-inch cake pans. Bake for 25 minutes. Cool thoroughly before removing from the pans.

Mix the strawberries and yogurt together in a bowl. Spoon onto wedges of sponge cake.

Makes 16 servings

One serving = 128 calories
           2 g protein
           31 g carbohydrate
           3 g fat
           161 mg sodium

One serving = 1 starch/bread + 1 fruit

Macadamia Pound Cake

½ cup margarine or butter
¾ cup sugar
4 large eggs
1 teaspoon vanilla extract
2 cups all-purpose flour
2 teaspoons baking powder
½ cup finely chopped
    macadamia nuts

Preheat the oven to 325°F. Beat the margarine, sugar, and eggs together until light and creamy. Add the vanilla, flour, and baking powder. Mix until the batter is smooth. Stir in the nuts. Pour the batter into an oiled and floured 9″ × 4″ loaf pan. Bake for about 1 hour or until the cake is browned and pulls away from sides of pan.

Makes 12 servings

One serving = 219 calories
           2 g protein
           31 g carbohydrate
           12 g fat
           218 mg sodium

One serving = 1 starch/bread + 1 fruit + 2 fat

Chocolate Chip Snack Cake

½ cup vegetable oil
⅓ cup honey
1 large egg
½ cup rolled oats
1 cup whole-wheat flour
1 tablespoon baking powder
½ cup semisweet chocolate chips
¾ cup skim milk

Preheat the oven to 350°F. Cream together the oil, honey, and egg. Add the oats, flour, baking powder, chocolate chips, and milk. Stir to blend thoroughly. Pour the batter into an oiled 8-inch square pan. Bake for about 30–35 minutes.

Makes 12 servings

One serving = 207 calories
4 g protein
28 g carbohydrate
8 g fat
347 mg sodium

One serving = 1 starch/bread + 1 fruit + 1 fat

Krumkaken
(Swedish Curled Cakes)

½ cup plain low-fat yogurt
1 large egg yolk
1 tablespoon sugar
½ teaspoon lemon extract
½ cup all-purpose flour

Combine all the ingredients in a bowl and beat until smooth. Pour about 1 tablespoon batter onto a hot oiled krumkaken or curled-cake iron over heat (see note). When the edges are dry, in about 1 minute, turn to brown the other side. Remove the cake from the iron and *quickly* wrap it around a cone or the handle of a wooden spoon. Cool.

Makes 10 cakes

Note: The batter can also be poured onto a hot oiled pancake griddle. When the edges look "dry," turn each thin cake to brown the other side. Remove from the griddle and *quickly* roll the cake around the handle of a wooden spoon.

One serving of 4 cakes = 83 calories
                        2 g protein
                        21 g carbohydrate
                        2 g fat
                        109 mg sodium

One serving = 1 starch/bread

Zucchini Cupcakes

½ cup vegetable oil
½ cup sugar
1 large egg
½ cup unsweetened applesauce
2 cups all-purpose flour
2 teaspoons baking powder
½ teaspoon baking soda
1 teaspoon ground cinnamon
½ teaspoon ground nutmeg
1 cup grated zucchini
½ cup raisins

Preheat the oven to 350°F. Cream the oil, sugar, and egg together. Add the rest of the ingredients and mix well. Fill paper-lined cupcake pans three-quarters full of batter. Bake for 15–20 minutes, until browned.

Makes 18 cupcakes

One cupcake = 173 calories
　　　　　　　2 g protein
　　　　　　　28 g carbohydrate
　　　　　　　7 g fat
　　　　　　　184 mg sodium

One cupcake = 1 starch/bread + 1 fruit + 1 fat

E a s y   C h e e s e c a k e

1 cup graham cracker crumbs
¼ cup margarine or butter,
    melted
1 32-ounce carton low-fat
    vanilla yogurt
2 tablespoons sugar
3 tablespoons cornstarch
½ teaspoon almond extract
2 large eggs

Preheat the oven to 425°F. Toss together the graham cracker crumbs and margarine. Press the mixture into the bottom of a 9-inch springform pan. Combine the yogurt, sugar, cornstarch, almond extract, and eggs in a bowl. Mix with a wire whip until well blended. Pour the batter into the pan. Bake for 50–60 minutes or until the center is set. Cool and refrigerate until serving time.

Makes 12 servings

One serving = 174 calories
                6 g protein
                22 g carbohydrate
                6 g fat
                339 mg sodium

One serving = 1 starch/bread + ½ milk + 1 fat

Yogurt Cheesecake

¾ cup honey crunch wheat germ
or graham cracker crumbs
2 tablespoons margarine, melted
½ pound low-fat cream cheese
8 ounces (1 cup) yogurt cheese
(see Index)
3 large egg yolks
2 tablespoons lemon yogurt
⅓ cup honey
6 large egg whites

Preheat the oven to 400°F. Combine the wheat germ and margarine in a bowl and toss together. Press into the bottom of a 10-inch springform pan. Beat together the cream cheese, yogurt cheese, egg yolks, lemon yogurt, and honey until smooth. In a separate bowl, beat the egg whites until stiff peaks form. Fold the egg yolk mixture into the egg white mixture.

Place the cake in the oven, immediately reduce the temperature to 300°F, and bake for 1 hour. Turn off the heat and leave the cheesecake in the oven for 2 hours longer. Cool for 1–2 hours at room temperature before refrigerating.

Makes 18 servings

One serving = 261 calories
9 g protein
27 g carbohydrate
16 g fat
457 mg sodium

One serving = 1 low-fat protein + 1 fruit + ½ starch/bread + 2 fat

French Bread Pudding

4 slices whole-wheat bread or
*   raisin bread*
2 large eggs
2 cups skim milk
¼ cup honey, sugar, or maple
*   syrup*
1 teaspoon vanilla extract
¼ teaspoon ground nutmeg

Preheat the oven to 350°F. Cut the bread into cubes. Place the cubes in a lightly oiled 1-quart baking dish. Combine the eggs, milk, honey, and vanilla in a mixing bowl or blender. Blend well and pour over the bread. Sprinkle the nutmeg on top. Bake for 30–40 minutes or until a knife inserted in the center comes out clean.

Makes 4 servings

One serving = 189 calories
                9 g protein
                37 g carbohydrate
                3 g fat
                408 mg sodium

One serving = 1 starch/bread + 1 fruit + ½ milk

Variation: Pineapple Bread Pudding
Add 1 6¼-ounce can juice-packed crushed pineapple to the bread in the baking dish. Reduce the milk to 1½ cups and proceed as directed. Use ¼ teaspoon almond extract instead of vanilla if desired.
One serving = 1 starch/bread + 1½ fruit

Rice Pudding

½ cup white rice
¾ cup water
2 cups skim milk
¼ cup sugar
1 teaspoon vanilla extract
½ cup raisins

Cook the rice in ¾ cup water over medium heat until tender, about 45 minutes. Add the skim milk and sugar. Cook slowly over low heat until thickened, about 30 minutes. Cool. Add the vanilla and raisins and spoon into six serving dishes.

Makes 6 servings

One serving = 189 calories
4 g protein
28 g carbohydrate
2 g fat
293 mg sodium

One serving = 1 starch/bread + 1 fruit + ½ milk

Tapioca Pudding

3 tablespoons tapioca
¼ cup honey or sugar
2 cups skim milk
1 large egg
1 teaspoon vanilla extract

Combine the tapioca, honey, and milk in a saucepan. Let stand for 10 minutes to soften the tapioca. (If pearl tapioca is used, increase the tapioca to ¼ cup and let stand for at least 2 hours before cooking.) Add the egg and beat to blend thoroughly. Bring to a full boil over medium heat, stirring constantly, about 5–7 minutes. Remove from the heat and stir in the vanilla. Pour into serving dishes and cool.

Makes 4 servings

One serving = 191 calories
                6 g protein
                27 g carbohydrate
                2 g fat
                381 mg sodium

One serving = 1 starch/bread + ½ milk + 1 fruit

B a k e d   C u s t a r d

4 large eggs
2 cups skim milk
½ teaspoon vanilla extract
2 tablespoons sugar
Ground nutmeg

Preheat the oven to 350°F. Beat the eggs until light and lemon colored. Stir in the milk, vanilla, and sugar. Divide the mixture among four custard cups or pour into a 1-quart glass casserole dish. Sprinkle with ground nutmeg. Set the custard cups or casserole dish into a pan of hot water; the water should come halfway up the sides of the cups. Bake for 30–40 minutes, until a dinner knife inserted in the center comes out clean. Remove the cups or dish from the water bath and cool for at least 1 hour before serving.

Makes 4 servings

One serving = 184 calories
            12 g protein
            18 g carbohydrate
            6 g fat
            207 mg sodium

One serving = 1 medium-fat protein + ½ milk + 1 fruit

Applesauce Brownies

⅓ cup vegetable oil
½ cup unsweetened applesauce
½ cup unsweetened cocoa
    powder
½ cup sugar
1 cup all-purpose flour
1 teaspoon baking powder
½ teaspoon baking soda
2 large eggs
1 teaspoon vanilla extract
¼ cup chopped nuts

Preheat the oven to 375°F. Combine the oil, applesauce, and cocoa in a bowl. Add the sugar and stir until dissolved. Add the flour, baking powder, baking soda, and eggs. Blend in the vanilla. Pour the batter into a greased and floured 9-inch square pan. Sprinkle on the nuts. Bake for about 30 minutes or until the crust is set but the edges are not dried out. Cut into 2-inch squares.

Makes 16 brownies

One brownie = 165 calories
            3 g protein
            27 g carbohydrate
            7 g fat
            84 mg sodium

One brownie = 1 starch/bread + 1 fat + 1 fruit

Guiltless Brownies

3 tablespoons unsweetened
    cocoa powder
¼ cup vegetable oil
2 very ripe bananas
½ cup sugar
2 large eggs
1 cup whole-wheat flour
½ cup chopped nuts

Preheat the oven to 350°F. Combine the cocoa, oil, and bananas in a food processor or blender. Puree until smooth. Combine the sugar, eggs, flour, and banana mixture in a mixing bowl. Beat until blended, then stir in the nuts. Pour the batter into a lightly oiled 13″ × 9″ baking pan and bake for 15–20 minutes or until done, when toothpick inserted into center comes out clean. Cut into 2¼-inch squares when cool.

Makes 24 brownies

One brownie = 115 calories
            2 g protein
            16 g carbohydrate
            5 g fat
            104 mg sodium

One brownie = 1 starch/bread + 1 fat

Zucchini Carrot Bars

½ cup vegetable oil
½ cup honey
2 large eggs
1 cup shredded zucchini
1 cup shredded carrot
2 cups whole-wheat flour
2 teaspoons baking powder
½ teaspoon ground nutmeg
1 teaspoon ground cinnamon
¼ teaspoon ground ginger
½ cup raisins
½ cup chopped walnuts
1-2 tablespoons frozen orange
    juice concentrate

Preheat the oven to 350°F. Cream together the vegetable oil, honey, and eggs until light and fluffy. Add the remaining ingredients except the concentrate and mix well. Spread into a lightly oiled 13″ × 9″ pan. Bake for 35–40 minutes, until toothpick inserted into center comes out clean. Cool in the pan. Glaze with orange juice concentrate before cutting into bars.

Makes 24 bars

One bar = 251 calories
        4 g protein
        32 g carbohydrate
        11 g fat
        390 mg sodium

One bar = 1 starch/bread + 1 fruit + 1 vegetable + 2 fat

Peanut Butter Chocolate Chip Cookies

½ cup vegetable oil
⅓ cup smooth peanut butter
⅓ cup brown sugar, packed
1 teaspoon vanilla extract
1 large egg
1 cup whole-wheat flour
2 teaspoons baking powder
¼ teaspoon baking soda
*½ cup miniature semisweet
    chocolate chips*
Sesame seeds

Preheat the oven to 375°F. Cream together the oil, peanut butter, brown sugar, vanilla, and egg until fluffy. Stir in the flour, baking powder, and baking soda. Add the chocolate chips and mix well (you may have to add 2 tablespoons water if the dough is dry). Shape the dough into walnut-size balls and place on lightly oiled baking sheets. Flatten with a fork or the bottom of a glass. Sprinkle sesame seeds on top for nutty flavor. Bake for 10–15 minutes, until browned.

Makes 36 cookies

One cookie = 135 calories
            4 g protein
            17 g carbohydrate
            8 g fat
            71 mg sodium

One cookie = 1 starch/bread + 1 fat

Chocolate
Chocolate Chip Cookies

¾ *cup vegetable oil*
⅔ *cup sugar*
1 *large egg*
1 *teaspoon baking powder*
½ *teaspoon baking soda*
1½ *cups all-purpose flour*
⅓ *cup unsweetened cocoa*
    powder
¼ *cup chopped walnuts*
½ *cup semisweet chocolate chips*

Beat together the oil, sugar, and egg. Add the rest of the ingredients and stir to blend well. Let stand for 10 minutes. Drop by spoonfuls, about 1 inch apart, onto a lightly oiled baking sheet. Bake for 12–15 minutes, until browned.

Makes 36 cookies

One cookie = 106 calories
            2 g protein
            18 g carbohydrate
            6 g fat
            124 mg sodium

One cookie = 1 starch/bread + 1 fat

Spritz Cookies

¾ cup margarine or butter
½ cup sugar
2 large egg yolks
½ teaspoon almond extract
2 cups all-purpose flour
½ teaspoon baking powder
Chopped nuts, sesame seeds,
    poppy seeds, or colored
    sugar crystals

Preheat the oven to 375°F. Cream the margarine, sugar, and egg yolks together until light. Add the almond extract. Gradually blend in the flour and baking powder. Chill the dough for 3 hours. Fill a cookie press fitted with the design plate of your choice. Form cookies on an ungreased cookie sheet and decorate with chopped nuts, sesame seeds, poppy seeds, or colored sugar crystals. Bake for about 10 minutes, until browned. Cool on a rack.

Makes 48 cookies

One cookie = 98 calories
            1 g protein
            6 g carbohydrate
            4 g fat
            51 mg sodium

One cookie = 1 starch/bread + 1 fat

White Chocolate Macadamia Cookies

¾ cup margarine
½ cup sugar
2 large eggs
1 teaspoon vanilla extract
1½ cups all-purpose flour
2 teaspoons baking powder
½ teaspoon baking soda
½ cup white chocolate pieces
½ cup chopped macadamia
       nuts, toasted

Preheat the oven to 375°F. Cream together the margarine, sugar, eggs, and vanilla. Add the rest of the ingredients and mix well. Drop by rounded teaspoonfuls, about 1 inch apart, onto a lightly oiled baking sheet. Bake for 10–15 minutes or until browned.

Makes 36 cookies

One cookie = 154 calories
             1 g protein
             18 g carbohydrate
             6 g fat
             74 mg sodium

One cookie = 1 starch/bread + 2 fat

Black Walnut Cookies

¾ cup vegetable oil
1 cup sugar
1 large egg
2 cups whole-wheat flour
½ teaspoon baking soda
⅓ cup unsweetened apple juice
   or water
1 cup chopped black walnuts

Cream the oil, sugar, and egg together in a bowl until smooth. Add the flour, baking soda, juice, and walnuts. Mix until blended. Drop by teaspoonfuls, about 1 inch apart, onto a lightly oiled baking sheet. Bake for 10–15 minutes, until browned.

Makes 36 cookies

One cookie = 103 calories
            2 g protein
            19 g carbohydrate
            8 g fat
            212 mg sodium

One cookie = 1 starch/bread + 1 fat

Peanut Butter Cookies

½ cup smooth peanut butter
¼ cup vegetable oil
1 cup packed brown sugar
1 teaspoon vanilla extract
1 large egg
1½ cups whole-wheat flour
2 teaspoons baking soda

Preheat the oven to 350°F. Cream together the peanut butter and vegetable oil in a bowl. Add the brown sugar, vanilla, and egg. Beat well. Add the flour and baking soda and blend thoroughly. Shape the dough into walnut-size balls and place, about 1 inch apart, on an ungreased baking sheet. Flatten with a fork or the bottom of a glass. Bake for 15 minutes.

Makes 24 cookies

One cookie = 96 calories
        2 g protein
        13 g carbohydrate
        4 g fat
        89 mg sodium

One cookie = 1 starch/bread + 1 fat

Gingerbread Cookies

1 cup margarine or butter
½ cup sugar
½ cup molasses
1 large egg
½ teaspoon baking soda
3½ cups all-purpose flour
1½ teaspoons ground ginger
1 teaspoon ground cinnamon

Preheat the oven to 375°F. Cream together the margarine, sugar, molasses, and egg. Add the baking soda, flour, ginger, and cinnamon. Mix until smooth. Refrigerate for 2 hours or overnight. Roll out ⅛ inch thick on a lightly floured surface. Cut with a cookie cutter. Place on an ungreased baking sheet and bake for 12–15 minutes, until browned.

Makes 48 gingerbread cookies

One serving of 2 cookies = 164 calories
2 g protein
21 g carbohydrate
8 g fat
114 mg sodium

One serving = 1 starch/bread + 2 fat

Oatmeal Cookies

1 cup vegetable oil
1 cup brown sugar, packed
1 cup whole-wheat flour
2 cups unbleached flour
¼ teaspoon salt
1 teaspoon baking soda
⅓ cup nonfat dry milk
2½ cups rolled oats
1 teaspoon vanilla extract
¾ cup water
1 large egg

Preheat the oven to 350°F. Cream the oil and brown sugar together in a bowl. Stir together the flours, salt, baking soda, dry milk, and oats. Add to the creamed mixture along with the vanilla, water, and egg. Beat thoroughly. Drop by teaspoonfuls, about 1 inch apart, onto a lightly oiled baking sheet. Bake for 5–8 minutes, until browned.

Makes 36 cookies

One cookie = 136 calories
            2 g protein
            17 g carbohydrate
            7 g fat
            62 mg sodium

One cookie = 1 starch/bread + 1 fat

Variations:

Oatmeal Spice: Add 1½ teaspoons ground cinnamon, ½ teaspoon ground nutmeg, and ¼ teaspoon ground cloves to the flour mixture. Stir in ½ cup chopped nuts.
One cookie = 184 calories

One cookie = 1 starch/bread + 2 fat

Oatmeal Raisin: Prepare as directed, but add ½ cup raisins instead of nuts to the batter.
One cookie = 142 calories

One cookie = 1 starch/bread + 1 fat

Oatmeal Chocolate Chip: Add 1 cup (6 ounces) semisweet chocolate chips to the basic recipe.
One cookie = 169 calories

One cookie = 1 starch/bread + 2 fat

Oatmeal Peanut Butter: Add 1 cup peanut butter to the basic recipe.
One cookie = 177 calories

One cookie = 1 starch/bread + 2 fat

Tofu   Peanut   Butter – Oatmeal Cookies

1 block soft tofu, drained
⅓ cup smooth peanut butter
¼ cup margarine or butter at
    room temperature
½ cup honey
1 teaspoon vanilla extract
1 cup all-purpose flour
2 teaspoons baking powder
1 cup old-fashioned rolled oats
½ cup chopped walnuts

Preheat the oven to 350°F. In a large bowl, cream the tofu, peanut butter, margarine, honey, and vanilla. Add the flour, baking powder, oats, and walnuts and beat thoroughly. Drop by teaspoonfuls about 2 inches apart onto an ungreased cookie sheet. Bake for 20–25 minutes, until browned.

Makes about 18 cookies

One cookie = 265 calories
              9 g protein
              28 g carbohydrate
              13 g fat
              239 mg sodium

One cookie = 1 starch/bread + 1 low-fat protein + 1 fruit + 2 fat

Crunchy Cereal Bar

¼ cup margarine or butter
⅓ cup brown sugar, packed
1 large egg
2 cups crumbled shredded wheat
*   biscuits*
½ cup chopped walnuts
1 cup raisins or chopped pitted
*   dates*

In a microwave-safe dish, combine the margarine and brown sugar. Microwave on HIGH for about 1 minute to melt the margarine. Beat in the egg when the sugar mixture has cooled, about 5 minutes. Add the shredded wheat, walnuts, and raisins. Stir until well mixed. Pat into the bottom of a 5-inch square microwave-safe dish. Microwave on HIGH for 4–6 minutes. Let stand for at least 10 minutes before cutting into bars.

To prepare in a conventional oven, preheat oven to 375°F. Cream together margarine and brown sugar. Beat in egg and add rest of ingredients. Pat mixture into bottom of an 8-inch square pan. Bake for 15–18 minutes or until the top is browned. Let stand for 5 minutes before cutting into bars.

Makes 18 bars

One bar = 198 calories
        2 g protein
        29 g carbohydrate
        12 g fat
        87 mg sodium

One bar = 1 starch/bread + 1 fruit + 2 fat

Granola Bars

⅓ *cup vegetable oil*
⅓ *cup brown sugar, packed*
¼ *cup molasses*
1 *6-ounce can frozen orange*
    juice concentrate, defrosted
2 *cups whole-wheat flour*
1 *teaspoon baking soda*
1 *teaspoon ground cinnamon*
½ *teaspoon ground ginger*
½ *cup rolled oats*
½ *cup chopped raisins*
½ *cup chopped dried apricots*
½ *cup sunflower seeds*
½ *cup wheat germ*
2 *tablespoons sesame seeds*

Preheat the oven to 350°F. Cream the oil, brown sugar, and molasses together in a bowl. Add the orange juice concentrate. Combine the flour, baking soda, cinnamon, and ginger; blend into the creamed mixture. Stir in the oats, raisins, apricots, sunflower seeds, wheat germ, and sesame seeds. Pour into a greased 13″ × 9″ pan. Bake for 30 minutes or until brown. Cut into bars.

Makes 24 bars

One bar = 140 calories
          3 g protein
          22 g carbohydrate
          5 g fat
          48 mg sodium

One bar = 1 starch/bread + ½ fruit + 1 fat

Apple Cheese Dessert Squares

5 *cups sliced peeled apples*
1 *tablespoon fresh lemon juice*
½ *cup sugar*
½ *teaspoon ground cinnamon*
½ *cup sifted all-purpose flour*
¼ *teaspoon salt*
¼ *cup margarine or butter*
½ *cup grated cheddar cheese*

Preheat the oven to 350°F. Fill a pie pan or shallow baking dish with the apples; sprinkle with lemon juice and ¼ cup of the sugar. Mix together the cinnamon, flour, salt, and remaining sugar. Cut in the margarine with a fork or pastry blender until the mixture is granular. Stir in the cheese. Spread the mixture over the apples. Bake until the apples are tender, about 40 minutes. Cool before cutting. Serve with vanilla yogurt if desired.

Makes 6 servings

One serving = 195 calories
4 g protein
28 g carbohydrate
7 g fat
287 mg sodium

One serving = 1 fruit + 1 starch/bread + 1 fat

Apple Crisp

3 apples, peeled, cored, and
   sliced
¼ cup rolled oats
1 tablespoon all-purpose flour
1 tablespoon margarine or
   butter, cut into small pieces
1 tablespoon sugar
½ teaspoon ground cinnamon

Preheat the oven to 350°F. Place the apple slices in an oiled
8-inch square baking pan. Combine the oats, flour, margarine, sugar, and cinnamon in a mixing bowl. Stir with a fork
until crumbly. Sprinkle over the apple slices. Bake for 20–25
minutes, until browned. Serve with vanilla yogurt if desired.

Makes 4 servings

One serving = 229 calories
               2 g protein
               31 g carbohydrate
               4 g fat
               179 mg sodium

One serving = 1 starch/bread + 2 fruit + 1 fat

Baked Apples

2 cooking apples
Orange juice
2 tablespoons raisins
Ground cinnamon
½ cup unsweetened apple juice
1 teaspoon cornstarch

Preheat the oven to 350°F. Peel and core the apples. Brush with orange juice on the peeled surface. Stuff the cavities with raisins. Sprinkle on some cinnamon. Place the apples in a shallow baking pan. Combine the apple juice and cornstarch until smooth. Pour into the bottom of the pan. Bake for 25–30 minutes or until a fork pierces the surface easily. Serve warm or cold with the sauce.

Makes 2 servings

One serving = 74 calories
0 g protein
19 g carbohydrate
0 g fat
0 mg sodium

One serving = 2 fruit

Baked Bananas in Strawberry Sauce

4 very ripe small bananas,
  unpeeled
1 cup sliced strawberries
1 tablespoon cornstarch or
  arrowroot
2 tablespoons water
2 tablespoons low-sugar orange
  marmalade
½ teaspoon rum extract
Strips of orange peel for garnish

Preheat the oven to 400°F. Trim about ½ inch off the ends of the bananas. Cut a slit down the length of the banana through the skin. Place the bananas on a baking sheet and bake for 15 minutes (the skin will turn brown).

Meanwhile, put the strawberries into a saucepan. Blend the cornstarch and water until smooth and add to the strawberries. Bring to a boil over high heat. Boil for 1 minute or until thick. Stir in the orange marmalade and rum extract. Pour into a serving dish.

Remove the bananas from the oven and let cool. Remove the bananas from the skins and place them in the sauce. Coat the bananas with the sauce and garnish with orange peel. Serve immediately.

Makes 8 servings

One serving = 74 calories
                1 g protein
                14 g carbohydrate
                1 g fat
                87 mg sodium

One serving = 1 fruit

Blueberry Crumble

1 cup fresh or frozen blueberries
¼ cup rolled oats
¼ cup all-purpose flour
1 tablespoon brown sugar,
    packed
½ teaspoon ground cinnamon
1 tablespoon margarine or butter

Place the blueberries in a microwave-safe dish. Combine the rest of the ingredients in a bowl. Blend with a fork until the mixture resembles granola in texture. Pour over the blueberries. Microwave on HIGH for 8–10 minutes or until the blueberries bubble around the oatmeal topping.

To prepare in a conventional oven, divide the ingredients between two 3-inch pyrex cups and bake at 375°F until the oatmeal crust is browned, about 15 minutes.

Makes 2 servings

One serving = 169 calories
    2 g protein
    28 g carbohydrate
    7 g fat
    91 mg sodium

One serving = 1 fruit + 1 starch/bread + 1 fat

Grapefruit Delight

1 large grapefruit
¼ cup honey crunch wheat germ
⅛ teaspoon ground cinnamon

Cut the grapefruit in half crosswise. Loosen each section with a knife. Place the grapefruit halves on a large micro-wave-safe round plate. Sprinkle on the wheat germ and cin-namon. Microwave on HIGH for 5–7 minutes or until heated through or broil 6 inches from the heat for 3–4 minutes or until brown on top.

Makes 2 servings

One serving = 130 calories
2 g protein
22 g carbohydrate
1 g fat
79 mg sodium

One serving = 1 fruit + 1 starch/bread

Peach Melba

*3 fresh peaches, peeled and
     halved, or 6 peach halves
     canned in juice*
⅓ cup low-fat vanilla yogurt
*½ cup raspberries, pureed (see
     note)*

Place each peach half in a serving dish. Spoon about 1 tablespoon yogurt over each peach half. Pour on the raspberry puree.

Makes 6 servings

Note: If the puree needs to be sweetened, add sugar substitute before serving.

One serving = 62 calories
          1 g protein
          13 g carbohydrate
          0 g fat
          37 mg sodium

One serving = 1 fruit

Poached Pears
with Chocolate Sauce

3 fresh pears, peeled, halved
  lengthwise, and cored
2 cups unsweetened apple juice
1 3-inch stick cinnamon
¼ cup skim milk
3 tablespoons unsweetened
  cocoa powder
1 tablespoon cornstarch
1½ tablespoons sugar

Place the pears in a saucepan. Add the apple juice and cinnamon stick. Bring to a boil, reduce the heat, and simmer, covered, for 15 minutes or until the pears are tender.

Combine the milk, cocoa, cornstarch, and sugar in another saucepan. Stir to mix well, then cook over medium heat until thick, about 5 minutes. Place the pears in a serving dish and drizzle with chocolate sauce. Serve immediately.

Makes 6 servings

One serving = 112 calories
                1 g protein
                35 g carbohydrate
                1 g fat
                46 mg sodium

One serving = 2 fruit

S t r a w b e r r i e s   R o m a n o f f

*1 cup vanilla yogurt cheese (see
    Index)*
1 teaspoon orange extract
2 cups fresh strawberries

Beat the yogurt cheese and orange extract together with a
wire whip until blended. Wash and hull the strawberries. Pour
the yogurt cheese mixture over the strawberries and refrigerate for at least 1 hour before serving.

Makes 4 servings

One serving = 92 calories
            3 g protein
            19 g carbohydrate
            1 g fat
            78 mg sodium

One serving = 1 fruit + 1 low-fat milk

Cream-Filled Strawberries

> 18 large strawberries
> 1 cup yogurt cheese (see Index)
> ½-1 cup skim milk
> ½ 4-ounce package vanilla-
>   flavor instant pudding
> 1 teaspoon almond extract

Cut the stem ends off the strawberries so they sit flat on a serving platter. Cut a deep X into the top of each strawberry with a sharp knife. Spread the strawberry apart with your fingertips to make "petals." Set aside. Combine the yogurt cheese, ½ cup skim milk, the instant pudding, and almond extract in a bowl. Beat with a wire whip or mixer until smooth, like whipped cream. (Extra milk may be needed to make it thin enough to push through a pastry bag.) Spoon the mixture into a pastry bag fitted with a large tip. Pipe yogurt cheese cream into each strawberry. Cover and refrigerate until ready to serve.

Makes 6 servings

One serving of 3 strawberries = 112 calories
                               5 g protein
                               16 g carbohydrate
                               4 g fat
                               209 mg sodium

One serving = 1 fruit + 1 low-fat protein

F r u i t   C o m p o t e

1 16-ounce can juice-packed
  pear halves
1 16-ounce can juice-packed
  peach slices
1 8¼-ounce can pineapple
  chunks in juice
1 cup seedless green grapes
1 cup fresh or frozen blueberries
1 tablespoon honey
1 teaspoon ground cinnamon
¼ teaspoon ground nutmeg
⅛ teaspoon ground cloves

Preheat the oven to 350°F. Drain the canned fruits, reserving 1 cup juice. Arrange the fruit and berries in a 2-quart casserole dish. Combine the reserved juice, honey, and spices in a bowl. Pour over the fruit. Bake for 15 minutes. Serve warm with vanilla yogurt or Strawberry Topping (recipe follows).

Makes 12 servings

One serving = 74 calories
             0 g protein
             12 g carbohydrate
             0 g fat
             18 mg sodium

One serving = 1 fruit

Strawberry Topping

½ cup vanilla yogurt
¼ cup low-sugar strawberry jam
1 cup unsweetened frozen
    strawberries, defrosted

Beat together the yogurt, jam, and strawberries with a wire whip or blender. Use as a sauce over waffles, Fruit Compote (preceding recipe), or fruit salads.

Makes 1½ cups

One serving of ¼ cup = 28 calories
                        1 g protein
                        7 g carbohydrate
                        0 g fat
                        52 mg sodium

One serving = ½ fruit

Swedish Fruit Soup

3 cups mixed dried fruits
(apricots, peaches, pears,
and apples)
½ cup pitted prunes
½ cup raisins
6 cups water
2 tablespoons honey
1 3-inch stick cinnamon
¼ teaspoon ground mace
Plain yogurt

Combine all the ingredients except the yogurt in a saucepan. Bring to a boil and simmer, covered, for 1 hour or until the fruit is tender. Remove the cinnamon stick. Serve hot or cold with a spoonful of yogurt.

Makes 8 cups

One serving of ½ cup = 109 calories
0 g protein
19 g carbohydrate
0 g fat
28 mg sodium

One serving = 2 fruit

Gingered Fruit

2 apples, cored and cubed
2 pears, cored and cubed
1 17-ounce can juice-packed
     peach slices
1 teaspoon ground ginger
Ground nutmeg
Vanilla yogurt

Combine the apples, pears, and peach slices with the juice and ginger in a microwave-safe 2-quart casserole dish. Stir to blend in the ginger. Microwave on HIGH for 2 minutes. Top each serving with nutmeg and a tablespoon of vanilla yogurt.

Makes 8 servings

One serving = 73 calories
             0 g protein
             14 g carbohydrate
             0 g fat
             26 mg sodium

One serving = 1 fruit

Cinnamon Crunch Snack Mix

2 tablespoons margarine
1 tablespoon honey
1 tablespoon frozen orange juice
     concentrate
1½ teaspoons ground cinnamon
6 cups puffed rice cereal

Combine the margarine, honey, orange juice concentrate, and cinnamon in a microwave-safe bowl. Microwave on HIGH for 15–20 seconds. Add the cereal and stir to coat. Microwave on HIGH for 1–2 minutes or until the cereal no longer looks "wet." Serve hot or cold.

To prepare in a conventional oven, preheat the oven to 300°F. Melt the margarine in a 13″ × 9″ pan. Stir in the honey, frozen orange juice concentrate, and cinnamon. Add the cereal and mix well. Bake for 15–20 minutes or until crispy.

Makes 6 cups

One serving of 1 cup = 131 calories
                      3 g protein
                      20 g carbohydrate
                      6 g fat
                      59 mg sodium

One serving = 1 starch/bread + 1 fat

Zesty Corn 'n' Nuts

1 tablespoon margarine
2 teaspoons chili powder
Dash Tabasco sauce (optional)
2 cups popped popcorn
2 cups miniature shredded
    wheat or Chex cereal
½ cup pecan halves

Melt the margarine in a skillet. Stir in the chili powder and the Tabasco sauce if desired. Add the rest of the ingredients and stir to blend well. Pour into a serving bowl.

Makes 3½ cups

One serving of ½ cup = 170 calories
                  2 g protein
                  19 g carbohydrate
                  11 g fat
                  305 mg sodium

One serving = 1 starch/bread + 2 fat

BEVERAGES

Gazpacho Cocktail

3 cups tomato juice
1 slice onion
¼ green bell pepper
½ cucumber, peeled and seeds
      removed
2 sprigs fresh parsley
Dash Tabasco sauce

Process the ingredients in a blender until smooth. Chill and serve in small glasses with a lemon wedge.

Makes 6 servings

One serving = 18 calories
                 1 g protein
                 6 g carbohydrate
                 0 g fat
                 58 mg sodium

One serving = 1 vegetable

Vegetable Juice Cocktail

2 cups tomato juice
1 rib celery
1 carrot
3 sprigs fresh parsley
2 tablespoons fresh lemon juice
½ teaspoon Worcestershire sauce

Combine the ingredients in a blender and process until smooth. Pour over ice to serve.

Makes 3 servings

One serving = 21 calories
              2 g protein
              6 g carbohydrate
              0 g fat
              59 mg sodium

One serving = 1 vegetable

Banana Smoothy

¼ cup pineapple juice
1 ripe banana
3 ice cubes

Combine the ingredients in a blender and puree until smooth. Pour into champagne glasses. Serve with a pineapple chunk for garnish.

Makes 2 servings

One serving = 65 calories
            0 g protein
            13 g carbohydrate
            0 g fat
            11 mg sodium

One serving = 1 fruit

Banana Rum Cocktail

½ *ripe banana*
½ *cup pineapple juice*
¼ *teaspoon rum extract*

Combine the ingredients in a blender and process until smooth. Pour over ice to serve.

Makes 1 serving

One serving = 71 calories
0 g protein
14 g carbohydrate
0 g fat
27 mg sodium

One serving = 1 fruit

Cranberry Cooler

¾ cup low-calorie cranberry
*   juice*
¼ cup club soda
Lime wedge

Combine the cranberry juice and club soda in a tall glass.
Add ice and serve with lime.

Makes 1 serving

One serving = 58 calories
            0 g protein
          13 g carbohydrate
            0 g fat
         15 mg sodium

One serving = 1 fruit

Frosty Peach Nog

3 cups sliced peeled fresh
    peaches
2 cups low-fat plain yogurt
¼ cup honey
2 teaspoons fresh lemon juice
¼ teaspoon vanilla extract

Put all the ingredients into a blender and process on high speed until smooth. Pour into chilled glasses to serve.

Makes 4 servings

One serving = 110 calories
            4 g protein
            18 g carbohydrate
            3 g fat
            67 mg sodium

One serving = 1 fruit + ½ milk

Purple Passion

½ fresh peach, peeled and pitted
¼ cup grape juice
½ cup club soda
Dash fresh lime juice
3 ice cubes

Combine all the ingredients in a blender and process until smooth. Serve immediately.

Makes 1 serving

One serving = 61 calories
          0 g protein
          13 g carbohydrate
          0 g fat
          4 mg sodium

One serving = 1 fruit

Strawberry Cantaloupe Cooler

> 2 cups fresh strawberries
> 2 cups cubed cantaloupe
> 1 tablespoon honey
> 1 teaspoon vanilla extract
> 1 cup club soda

Combine the strawberries, cantaloupe, honey, and vanilla in a blender. Process until smooth. Add the club soda and serve over ice.

Makes 4 servings

One serving = 71 calories
          0 g protein
          20 g carbohydrate
          0 g fat
          22 mg sodium

One serving = 1 fruit

Strawberry Yogurt Drink

1 cup sliced strawberries
½ cup low-fat yogurt
½ banana
3 ice cubes
Strawberries for garnish

Combine the sliced strawberries, yogurt, banana, and ice cubes in a blender. Process until smooth. Pour into glasses and garnish each serving with a strawberry.

Makes 2 servings

One serving = 79 calories
2 g protein
12 g carbohydrate
1 g fat
31 mg sodium

One serving = 1 fruit

Tropical Splash

1 mango, peeled and pitted
½ banana
½ cup grapefruit juice

Combine the ingredients in a blender and process until smooth. Serve over ice in tall glasses.

Makes 2 servings

One serving = 69 calories
    0 g protein
    14 g carbohydrate
    0 g fat
    15 mg sodium

One serving = 1 fruit

INDEX